Food for Beginners

Everyday Cookbook

STAR
FIRE

This is a Star Fire book
First published in 2006

06 08 10 09 07

1 3 5 7 9 10 8 6 4 2

Star Fire is part of
The Foundry Creative Media Company Limited
Crabtree Hall, Crabtree Lane, Fulham, London, SW6 6TY

Visit our website: www.star-fire.co.uk

ISBN-10: 1-84451-533-8 ISBN-13: 978-1-84451-533-2
Special Edition: ISBN-10: 1-84451-576-1 ISBN-13: 978-1-84451-576-9

The CIP record for this book is available from the British Library.

Printed in China

ACKNOWLEDGEMENTS

Publisher and Creative Director: Nick Wells
Editorial Planning: Rosanna Singler
Design and Production: Chris Herbert, Mike Spender, Colin Rudderham and Claire Walker

Authors: Catherine Atkinson, Juliet Barker, Gina Steer, Vicki Smallwood,
Carol Tennant, Mari Mererid Williams, Elizabeth Wolf-Cohen and Simone Wright
Editorial: Sara Goulding and Sara Robson
Photography: Colin Bowling, Paul Forrester and Stephen Brayne
Home Economists and Stylists: Jacqueline Bellefontaine,
Mandy Phipps, Vicki Smallwood and Penny Stephens

All props supplied by Barbara Stewart at Surfaces

NOTE
Recipes using uncooked eggs should be avoided by infants,
the elderly, pregnant women and anyone suffering from an illness.

Contents

Techniques and Tips

Basic Recipes

Simple Soups & Easy Starters

Hassle-free Main Courses

Step-by-step Desserts

Entertaining

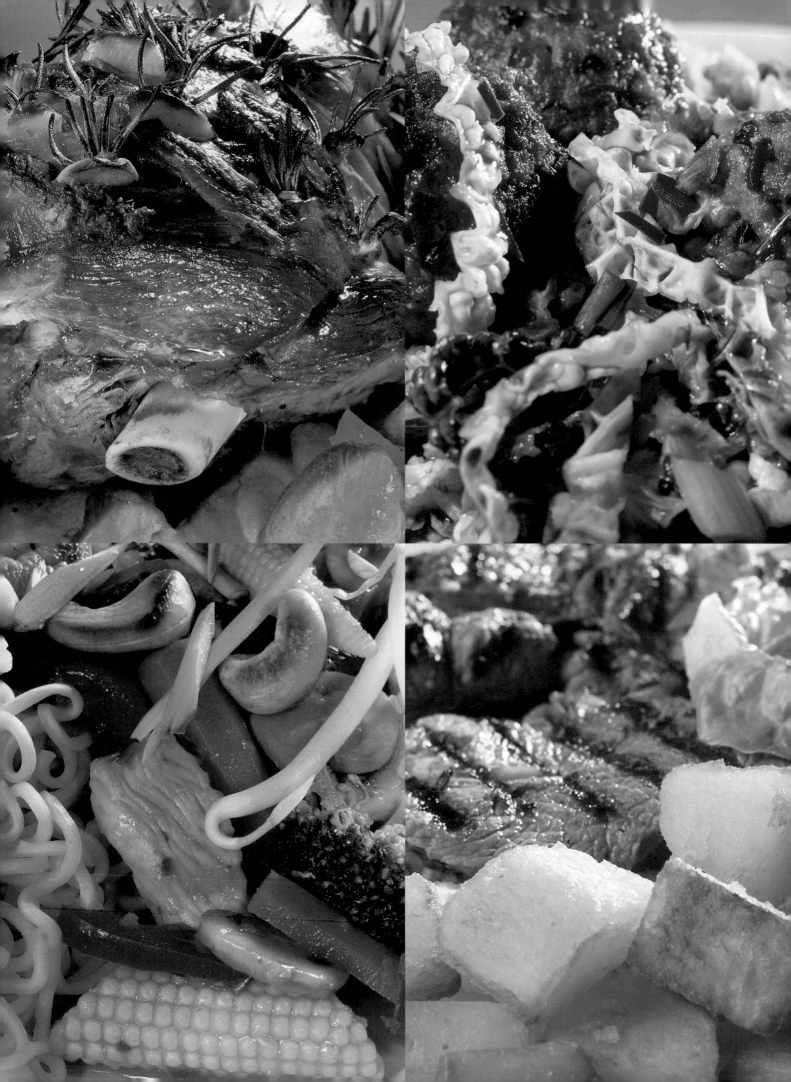

Techniques
& Tips

The key to cooking is having a good knowledge of the ingredients, how to decipher their quality and how to cook them properly. This section tells you everything you need to know about the different varieties of meat, fish, vegetables, rice and pasta.

Meat

Both home-grown and imported meat is readily available from supermarkets, butchers, farm shops and markets. Home-grown meat is normally more expensive than imported meat, often brought into the country frozen. Meat also varies in price depending on the cut. The more expensive and tender meats are usually those cuts that exercised less. They need a minimal amount of cooking and are suitable for roasting, grilling, griddling, frying and stir-frying. The cheaper cuts normally need longer, slower cooking and are used in casseroles and for stewing. Meat plays an important part in most people's diet, offering an excellent source of protein, B vitamins and iron.

When choosing meat, it is important to buy from a reputable source and to choose the correct cut for the cooking method. Look for meat that is lean without an excess of fat, is a good colour and has no unpleasant odour. If in doubt about the suitability of a cut, ask the butcher who should be happy to advise.

If buying frozen meat, allow to thaw before using. This is especially important for both pork and poultry. It is better to thaw meat slowly, lightly covered on the bottom shelf of the refrigerator. Use within 2–3 days of thawing, providing it has been kept in the refrigerator. If buying meat to freeze, do not freeze large joints in a home freezer as it will not be frozen quickly enough.

Store thawed or fresh meat out of the supermarket wrappings, on a plate, lightly covered with greaseproof or baking paper and then wrap with clingfilm if liked. Do not secure the paper tightly round the meat as it needs to breathe. Ensure that the raw meat juices do not drip onto cooked foods. The refrigerator needs to be at a temperature of 5°C.

Fresh meat such as joints, chops and steaks can be stored for up to three days. Mince, sausages and offal should be stored for only one day.

Different cultures and religion affect the way the meat has been killed and the carcass cut. The following is a description of different cuts of meat. They may be called by different names in different parts of the country.

Beef

When choosing beef, look for meat that is a good colour, with creamy yellow fat. There should be small flecks of fat (marbling) throughout, as this helps the meat to be tender. Avoid meat with excess gristle. Bright red beef means that the animal has been butchered recently, whereas meat that has a dark, almost purple, tinge is from meat that has been hung in a traditional manner. The darker the colour, especially with roasting joints, the more tender and succulent the beef will be.

Rib or fore rib – suitable for roasting. Sold either on or off the bone. Look for meat that is marbled for tenderness and succulence.

Topside – suitable for pot roasting, roasting or braising. A lean, tender cut from the hindquarter.

Sirloin – suitable for roasting, grilling, frying, barbecuing or griddling. Sold boned or off the bone. A lean and tender cut from the back.

T-bone steak – suitable for grilling, griddling, barbecuing or roasting. A tender, succulent cut taken from the fillet end of the sirloin.

Top rib – suitable for pot roasting or braising. Sold on or off the bone.

Fillet steak – suitable for grilling, frying, barbecuing or griddling. A whole fillet is used to make Châteaubriand, some say the best of all cuts. The most tender and succulent cut with virtually no fat. Comes from the centre of the sirloin.

Rump – suitable for grilling, frying, griddling or barbecuing. Not as tender as fillet of sirloin, but reputed to have more flavour.

Silverside – suitable for boiling and pot roasts. Used to be sold ready-salted but is now normally sold unsalted.

Flash-fry steaks – suitable for grilling, griddling or frying. Cut from the silverside, thick flank or topside.

Braising steak – chuck, blade or thick rib, ideal for all braising or stews. Sold either in pieces or ready diced.

Flank – suitable for braising or stewing. A boneless cut from the mid- to hindquarter.

Minute steaks – suitable for grilling or griddling. Cut from the flank, a thin steak and beaten to flatten.

Skirt – suitable for stewing or making into mince. A boneless, rather gristly cut.

Brisket – suitable for slow roasting or pot roasting. Sold boned and rolled and can be found salted.

Mince – suitable for meat sauces such as bolognese, also burgers, shepherd's pie and moussaka. Normally cut from clod, skirt, neck, thin rib or flank. Can be quite fatty. Steaks can also be minced if preferred to give a leaner mince. Sometimes referred to as ground beef.

Ox kidney – suitable for casseroles and stews. Strong flavour with a hard central core that is discarded.

Oxtail – suitable for casseroles or braising. Normally sold cut into small pieces.

Lamb

Lamb is probably at its best in the Spring, when the youngest lamb is available. It is tender to eat with a delicate flavour, and its flesh is a paler pink than the older lamb where the flesh is more red. The colour of the fat is also a good indication of age: young lamb fat is a very light, creamy colour. As the lamb matures, the fat becomes whiter and firmer.

Imported lamb also has firmer, whiter fat. Lamb can be fatty so take care when choosing. It used to be possible to buy mutton (lamb that is at least one year old), but this now tends to be available only in specialist outlets. It has a far stronger, almost gamey flavour and the joints tend to be larger.

Leg – suitable for roasting. Often sold as half legs and steaks cut from the fillet end. These can be grilled, griddled or barbecued. Steaks are very lean and need a little oil to prevent the meat from drying out.

Shank – suitable for braising. A cut off the leg.

Shoulder – suitable for roasting. Can be sold boned, stuffed and rolled. Is fattier than the leg and has more flavour.

Loin – suitable for roasting. Sold on or off the bone, and can be stuffed and rolled. Can also be cut into chops, often as double loin chops which are suitable for grilling, griddling and barbecuing.

Noisette – suitable for grilling, griddling or barbecuing. A small boneless chop cut from the loin.

Valentine steak – suitable for grilling, griddling or barbecuing. Cut from a loin chop.

Chump chop – suitable for grilling, griddling or barbecuing. Larger than loin chops and can be sold boneless.

Best end of neck – suitable for roasting, grilling or griddling. Sold as a joint or cutlets.

Neck fillet – suitable for grilling or griddling. Sold whole or diced.

Middle and scrag end – suitable for pot roasting, braising or stewing. A cheaper cut with a high ratio of fat and bone.

Breast – suitable for pot roast if boned, stuffed and rolled. Can be marinated and grilled or barbecued.

Mince – suitable for burgers, pies, meatballs and for stuffing vegetables such as peppers. From various cuts and is often fatty.

Liver – suitable for pan frying or grilling. Milder than ox or pig liver and cheaper than calves' liver.

Kidney – suitable for grilling, pan frying or casserole. Milder than ox or pig kidney and normally sold encased in suet that is discarded.

Pork

Pork should be pale pink in colour and slightly marbled with small flecks of fat. There should be a good layer of firm white fat with a thin elastic skin (rind) which can be scored before roasting to provide crackling. All cuts of pork are normally tender, as the pigs are slaughtered at an early age and nowadays are reared to be lean rather than fatty. Pork used to be well-cooked, if not over-cooked, due to the danger of the parasite trichina. This no longer applies, however, and it is now recommended that the meat is cooked less to keep it moist and tender.

Leg – suitable for roasting. Sold either on the bone or boned. Can be cut into chunks and braised or casseroled.

Steaks – suitable for grilling, frying, griddling or barbecue. A lean cut from the leg or the shoulder. Very tender but can be dry.

Fillet – sometimes called tenderloin and suitable for roasting, pan frying, griddling or barbecuing. A tender cut, often sold already marinated.

Loin – suitable for roasting as a joint or cut into chops. Often sold with the kidney intact.

Shoulder – suitable for roasting. Often referred to as hand and spring, and sold cubed for casseroles and stews. A fatty cut.

Spare ribs – suitable for barbecuing, casseroles and roasting. Sold either as 'Chinese' where thin ribs are marinated then cooked, or 'American Style' ribs which are larger.

Escalope – suitable for grilling, frying, griddling or barbecuing. Very lean and tender and requires very little cooking.

Mince – suitable for burgers, meatballs or similar recipes. Can be from several different cuts, but is often from the cheaper cuts and can be fatty.

Belly – suitable for grilling or roasting. Can be salted before cooking. Is generally used to provide streaky bacon and is perhaps the fattiest cut of all.

Liver – suitable for casseroles or frying. Stronger than lamb or calves' liver.

Kidney – suitable for casseroles or frying. Often sold as part of a loin chop. Stronger than lambs' kidneys.

Poultry & Game

Poultry relates to turkey, chicken, poussin, duck and geese. Most poultry is sold plucked, drawn and trussed. Due to extensive farming since the war, chicken in particular offers a good source of cheap meat. However, there is a growing movement to return to the more traditional methods of farming. Organically-grown chickens offer a far more succulent bird with excellent flavour, although they tend to be a little more expensive. Both home-grown and imported poultry, fresh and frozen are available. When buying fresh poultry, look for plump birds with a flexible breast bone, and no unpleasant odour or green tinge.

Frozen poultry should be rock hard with no ice crystals, as this could mean that the bird has thawed and been re-frozen. Avoid any produce where the packaging is damaged. When thawing, place in the refrigerator on a large plate and ensure that none of the juices drip onto other foods. Once thawed, remove all packaging, remove the giblets, if any, and reserve separately. Place on a plate and cover. Use within two days and ensure that the meat is thoroughly cooked and the juices run clear. Rest for 10 minutes before carving.

When storing fresh poultry, place on a plate and cover lightly, allowing air to circulate. Treat as thawed poultry: store for no longer than two days in the refrigerator, storing the giblets separately, and ensure that it is thoroughly cooked. Use within two days of cooking.

Poultry and game are low in saturated fat and provide a good source of protein as well as selenium, an antioxodant mineral. Remove the skin from poultry before eating if following a low-fat diet.

Poultry

Turkey – whole birds are suitable for roasting. Traditionally served at Christmas, although with all the different cuts now available, turkey is eaten throughout the year.

Crown – the whole bird with the legs removed.

Saddle – two turkey breast fillets, boned with the wings inserted.

Butterfly – the two breast fillets.

Breast roll – boned breast meat, rolled and tied or contained in a net.

Turkey portions are also available, ranging from breast steaks, diced thigh, escalopes, small whole breast fillets, drumsticks, wings and mince.

Chicken – suitable for all types of cooking: roasting, grilling, griddling, stewing, braising, frying and

barbecuing. Also available in many different breeds and varieties, offering a good choice to the consumer. There are many cuts of chicken readily available: breast, wing and leg quarters which are still on the bone, drumsticks, thighs, breast fillets, escalopes (boneless, skinless portions), diced and stir-fry strips as well as mince.

Capon – suitable for roasting. These are young castrated cockerels and are normally bred for their excellent flavour.

Broilers – these are older chickens which would be too tough to roast. Normally quite small birds about 1.6 kg/3½ lbs.

Poussin – suitable for roasting, grilling or casseroles. These are spring chickens and are 4–6 weeks old. They can be bought whole or spatchcocked – this is where the bird is split through the breast, opened up and secured on skewers. Normally serve two per person if small (450 g/1 lb) or one if larger (900 g/2 lb).

Guinea fowl – suitable for roasting or casseroles. Available all year round and about the same size as a pheasant, with a slightly gamey flavour. Most guinea fowl have already been hung and are sold ready for the table. When roasting, use plenty of fat or bacon as they can be dry.

Goose – suitable for roasting and often served as an alternative to turkey. Once dressed for the table, a goose will weigh around 4.5 kg/10 lb, but there is not much meat and this will serve around 6–8 people. It is very fatty, so pierce the skin well and roast on a trivet so the fat can be discarded or used for other cooking. Has a rich flavour, slightly gamey and a little like duck. Goose liver is highly prized and is used for foie gras.

Duck – suitable for roasting, grilling, griddling and casseroles. Ducklings are normally used for the table and are between six weeks to three months old; ducks are not normally eaten. Duck has an excellent flavour but it is a fatty bird, so cook on a trivet as for goose. Available fresh or frozen and on average weighs 1.75–2.75 kg/4–6 lb. Also available in cuts, as boneless breast fillets, ideal for grilling or griddling, and leg portions, suitable for casseroles. The meat is also used to make pâté. There are quite a few varieties available, with perhaps the best well-known being the Aylesbury. Long Island, Peking and Barbary are also popular varieties.

Game

Game describes birds or animals which are hunted, not farmed, although some, such as pheasant, quails and rabbits, are now being reared domestically. Most game has a stronger flavour than poultry and some is at it's best when 'high' and smelling quite strong. Game is not as popular as most meat or poultry and is an acquired taste. When buying game, it is important to know its age, as this dictates the method of cooking. Normally sold oven-ready, it is advisable to buy from a reputable source who can guarantee the quality.

Pigeon – suitable for casseroles or stews, although the breast from young pigeons can be fried or grilled. Sometimes classified as poultry. Not widely available, mainly from licensed game sources.

Pheasant – suitable for roasting or casseroles. Breast, which can be grilled, is also available. Pheasant needs to be well hung to give the best flavour.

Rabbit – suitable for casseroles, stews and can be roasted, or if young, fried. Also makes excellent pies and fricassée. Sold whole or in portions, both with and without the bone, and available both fresh and frozen. Frozen rabbit often comes from China. If a milder flavour is preferred, soak in cold salted water for two hours before using. Generally regarded as country food and not served as haute cuisine.

Hare – suitable for casseroles. The most well-known recipe is Jugged Hare, where the blood is used to thicken the dish. Has a strong, gamey flavour. If a milder flavour is preferred, soak in cold water for up to 24 hours. Available from reputable game dealers.

Venison – suitable for roasting, grilling, casseroles or making into sausages. The best joints for roasting are the saddle, haunch and shoulder, although the loin and fillet can also be used. All cuts benefit from marinating to help tenderise.

Other game which is less widely available includes partridge, grouse, quail, snipe and boar.

Vegetables & Salads

Vegetables add colour, texture, flavour and valuable nutrients to a meal. They play an important role in the diet, providing necessary vitamins, minerals and fibre. Vegetables are versatile: they can be served as an accompaniment to other dishes – they go well with meat, poultry and fish – or they can be used as the basis for the whole meal. There is a huge range of fresh vegetables on sale today in supermarkets, greengrocers and local markets. Also available is a growing selection of fresh organic produce, plus a wide variety of seasonal pick-your-own vegetables. For enthusiastic gardeners, a vast range of vegetable seeds are available. In addition, the increase of ethnic markets has introduced an extensive choice of exotic vegetables, such as chayote and breadfruit. With improved refrigeration and transport networks, vegetables are now flown around the world resulting in year-round availability.

Vegetables are classified into different groups: leaf vegetables; roots and tubers; beans, pods and shoots; bulb vegetables; fruit vegetables; brassicas; cucumbers and squashes; sea vegetables; and mushrooms.

Leaf Vegetables

This includes lettuce and other salad leaves, such as oakleaf, frisée, radicchio, lamb's lettuce and lollo rosso as well as rocket, spinach, Swiss chard and watercress. These are available all year round as most are now grown under glass. Many leaf vegetables, such as watercress and spinach, are delicious cooked and made into soups.

Roots and Tubers

This group includes beetroot, carrots, celeriac, daikon, Jerusalem artichokes, parsnips, potatoes, radish, salsify, scorzonera, sweet potatoes, swede, turnip and yam. Most are available all year round.

Beans, Pods and Shoots

This category includes all the beans, such as broad beans, French beans, mangetout and runner beans as well as peas, sugar snap peas and sweetcorn,

baby corn and okra. Shoots include asparagus, bamboo shoots, celery, chicory, fennel, globe artichokes and palm hearts. The majority are available all year round.

Bulb Vegetables

This is the onion family and includes all the different types of onion, from the common brown-skinned globe onion, Italian red onion and Spanish onion to shallots, pickling onions, pearl onions and spring onions. This category also includes leeks, chives and garlic. All are available throughout the year.

Fruit Vegetables

This group originates from hot climates like the Mediterranean and includes aubergines, avocados, chilli peppers, sweet peppers and tomatoes. These are available all year round but are more plentiful in the summer.

Brassicas

This is the cabbage family and includes all the different types of cabbage, broccoli, Brussels sprouts, cauliflower, curly kale, Chinese cabbage, pak choi and purple sprouting broccoli. Some of the cabbages are only seasonal, such as Savoy cabbage and red cabbage, while summer cabbages are available only during the summer months.

Cucumbers and Squashes

These vegetables are members of the gourd family and include cucumbers, gherkins, pumpkins and other squashes. There are two types of squash – summer squashes, which include courgettes, marrows, and pattypan squashes, and winter squashes such as pumpkins and butternut, acorn, gem and spaghetti squashes. Courgettes and cucumbers are available all year but pumpkins and other winter squashes and marrow are seasonal.

Sea Vegetables

The vegetables from this group may be quite difficult to find in supermarkets. The most readily available are seaweed (normally available dried) and sea kale.

Mushrooms and Fungi

This category includes all the different types of mushroom: the cultivated button mushrooms, chestnut mushrooms, large portobello or flat mushrooms and oyster and shiitake mushrooms, as well as wild mushrooms such as ceps, morels, chanterelles and truffles. Cultivated mushrooms are available throughout the year but wild ones are only around from late summer. If you collect your own wild mushrooms, make sure you correctly identify them before picking as some are very poisonous and can be fatal if eaten. Dried mushrooms are also available, including ceps, morels and oyster mushrooms. They add a good flavour to a dish, but need to be re-constituted before use.

Buying and Storage

When buying fresh vegetables, always look for ones that are bright and feel firm to the touch, and avoid any that are damaged or bruised. Choose onions and garlic that are hard and not sprouting and avoid ones that are soft as they may be damaged. Salad leaves and other leaf vegetables should be fresh, bright and crisp – do not buy any that are wilted, look limp or have yellow leaves. Vegetables like peas and beans do not keep for very long, so try to eat them as soon as possible after buying or picking. Most vegetables can be stored in a cool, dry place that is frost-free, such as the larder or garage. Green vegetables, fruit vegetables and salad leaves should be kept in the salad drawer of the refrigerator, while root vegetables, tuber vegetables and winter squashes should be kept in a cool, dark place. Winter squashes can be kept for several months if stored correctly.

Preparation

Always clean vegetables thoroughly before using. Brush or scrape off any dirt and wash well in cold water. Wash lettuce and other salad leaves gently under cold running water and tear rather than cut the leaves. Dry thoroughly in a salad spinner or on kitchen paper before use, otherwise the leaves tend to wilt. Spinach should be washed thoroughly to remove all traces of dirt, and you should cut off and discard any tough stalks and damaged leaves. Wash leaf vegetables and salad leaves well, then pull off and discard any tough stalks or outer leaves. Leeks need to be thoroughly cleaned before use to remove any grit and dirt. Most mushrooms just need wiping with a damp cloth. Prepare the vegetables just before cooking, as once peeled they lose nutrients. Do not leave them in water, as valuable water-soluble vitamins will be lost.

Cooking Techniques

Vegetables can be cooked in a variety of different ways, such as baking, barbecuing, blanching, boiling, braising, deep-frying, grilling, roasting, sautéing, steaming and stir-frying.

Boiling Always cook vegetables in a minimum amount of water and do not over-cook, or valuable nutrients will be lost. It is best to cut vegetables into even-sized pieces and briefly cook them in a small amount of water.

Blanching This means lightly cooking raw vegetables for a brief period of time. It is a method used to par-boil potatoes before frying or roasting, cabbage before braising and for cooking leaf vegetables such as spinach. Spinach should be cooked in only the water clinging to its leaves for 2–3 minutes, or until wilted. Blanching is also used to easily remove skins from tomatoes. Cut a small cross in the top of the tomato and place in a heatproof bowl. Cover with boiling water and leave for a few seconds, then drain and peel off the skin.

Braising This method is a slow way of cooking certain vegetables, notably cabbage and leeks. The vegetable is simmered for a long period of time in a small amount of stock or water.

Deep-frying This method is suitable for most vegetables except leaf. The vegetables can be cut into small pieces, coated in batter, then deep-fried briefly in hot oil.

Grilling When grilling and barbecuing peppers, aubergines and tomatoes, brush them with a little oil first as they quickly dry out. To remove the skins from peppers, cut the pepper in half lengthways and de-seed. Place the peppers skin-side up on the grill rack under a pre-heated hot grill and cook until the skins are blackened and blistered. Remove the peppers with tongs and place in a polythene bag, which will retain moisture. Seal and leave until the peppers are cool enough to handle. Once cool, remove from the bag and carefully peel away the blackened skin.

Roasting This method is suitable for vegetables such as fennel, courgettes, pumpkin, squash, peppers, garlic, aubergine and tomatoes. Cut the vegetables into even-sized chunks. Heat some oil in a roasting tin in a preheated oven at 200°C/400°F /Gas Mark 6. Put the vegetables in the hot oil, baste, and roast in the oven for 30 minutes. Garlic can be split into different cloves or whole heads of garlic can be roasted. It is best not to peel them until after cooked.

Steaming This is a great way to cook vegetables such as broccoli, cauliflower, beans, carrots, parsnips and peas. Fill a large saucepan with about 5 cm/2 inches of water. Cut the vegetables into even-sized pieces, place in a metal steamer or on a plate and lower into the saucepan, then cover and steam until tender. Do not let the water boil – it should be just simmering. Once tender, refresh under cold running water. Asparagus is best steamed and is traditionally cooked in an asparagus steamer.

Health and Nutrition

Vegetables contain many essential nutrients and are especially high in vitamins A, B and C. They contain important minerals, in particular iron and calcium, and are also low in fat, high in fibre and have low cholesterol value. Red and orange vegetables, such as peppers and carrots, and dark green vegetables, such as broccoli, are an essential part of the diet as they contain excellent anti-cancer properties as well as helping to prevent heart disease. Current healthy eating guidelines suggest that five portions of fruit and vegetables should be eaten per day, with vegetables being the more essential.

Pasta

How to Make Pasta
Home-made pasta has a light, almost silky texture and is different from the fresh pasta that you can buy vacuum-packed in supermarkets. It is also easy to make and little equipment is needed, just a rolling pin and a sharp knife. If you make pasta regularly it is perhaps worth investing in a pasta machine.

Basic Egg Pasta Dough
225 g/8 oz type 'oo' pasta flour, plus extra for dusting

1 tsp salt

2 eggs, plus 1 egg yolk

1 tbsp olive oil

1–3 tsp cold water

Sift the flour and salt into a mound on a work surface and make a well in the middle, keeping the sides high so that the egg mixture will not trickle out when added. Beat the eggs, yolk, oil and 1 teaspoon of water together. Add to the well, then gradually work in the flour, adding extra water if needed, to make a soft, not sticky dough. Knead on a lightly floured surface for 5 minutes, or until the dough is smooth and elastic. Wrap in clingfilm and leave for 20 minutes at room temperature.

Using a Food Processor
Sift the flour and salt into a food processor fitted with a metal blade. Add the eggs, yolk, oil and water and pulse-blend until mixed and the dough begins to come together, adding extra water if needed. Knead for 1–2 minutes, then wrap and rest as before.

Rolling Pasta by Hand
Unwrap the pasta dough and cut in half. Work with just half at a time and keep the other half wrapped in clingfilm. Place the dough on a lightly-floured work surface, then flatten and roll out. Always roll away from you, starting from the centre and giving the dough a quarter turn after each rolling. Sprinkle a little more flour over the dough if it starts to get sticky. Continue rolling and turning until the dough is as thin as possible, ideally 3 mm/⅛ inch thick.

Rolling Pasta by Machine
Always refer to the manufacturers' instructions before using. Clamp the machine securely and attach the handle. Set the rollers at their widest setting and sprinkle with flour. Cut the pasta dough into four pieces. Wrap three of them in clingfilm and reserve. Flatten the unwrapped dough slightly, then feed it through the rollers. Fold the strip of dough in three, rotate and feed through the rollers a second time. Continue to roll the dough, narrowing the roller setting by one notch every second time and flouring the rollers if the dough starts to get sticky. Only fold the dough the first time it goes through each roller width. If it gets too difficult to handle, cut the strip in half and work with one piece at a time. Fresh pasta should be dried slightly before cutting. Either drape over a wooden pole for five minutes or place on a tea towel sprinkled with a little flour for 10 minutes.

Shaping Up
When cutting and shaping freshly-made pasta, have several lightly-floured tea towels ready.

Farfalle Use a fluted pasta wheel to cut the pasta sheets into rectangles 2.5 x 5 cm/1 x 12 inches. Pinch the long sides of each rectangle in the middle to make a bow. Spread out on a floured tea towel and leave for 15 minutes.

Lasagne Trim the pasta sheets until neat and cut into lengths. Spread the sheets on tea towels sprinkled with flour.

Noodles If using a pasta machine, use the cutter attachment to produce tagliatelle or use a narrower one for spaghetti. To make by hand, sprinkle the rolled-out pasta with flour, then roll up like a Swiss roll and cut into thin slices. Unravel immediately after cutting. Leave over a wooden pole for five minutes to dry.

Ravioli Cut the rolled-out sheet of dough in half widthways. Cover one half. Brush the other sheet of dough with beaten egg. Place 1 teaspoon of filling in even rows, spacing them at 4 cm/1½ inch intervals. Remove the clingfilm from the reserved pasta sheet and, using a rolling pin, lift over the dough with the filling. Press down between the pockets to push out any air. Cut into squares. Leave on a floured tea towel for 45 minutes before cooking.

Variations

Flavoured pastas are simple and there are dozens of ways that you can change the flavour and colour of pasta.

Chilli Add 2 teaspoons of crushed, dried red chillies to the egg mixture.

Herb Stir 3 tablespoons of chopped fresh herbs into the flour.

Olive Blend 2 tablespoons of black olive paste with the egg mixture and omit the water.

Porcini Soak 15 g/½ oz dried porcini mushrooms in boiling water for 20 minutes. Drain and squeeze out as much water as possible, then chop finely. Add to the egg mixture.

Spinach Chop 75 g/3 oz cooked fresh spinach finely. Add to the egg mixture.

Dried Pasta Varieties

Buckwheat A gluten-free pasta made from buckwheat flour.

Coloured and flavoured pasta Varieties are endless, the most popular being spinach and tomato. Others include beetroot, herb, garlic, chilli, mushroom and black ink.

Durum wheat pasta Most readily available and may be made with or without eggs. Look for 'durum wheat' or 'pasta di semola di grano duro' on the packet, as pastas made from soft wheat tend to become soggy when cooked.

Wholewheat pasta Made with wholemeal flour, this has a higher fibre content than ordinary pasta. Wholewheat pasta takes longer to cook than the refined version.

Pasta Shapes

Long Pasta

Spaghetti Probably the best known type of pasta, spaghetti derives its name from the word 'spago' meaning string, which describes its round, thin shape perfectly.

Tagliatelle Most common type of ribbon noodle pasta. It is traditionally from Bologna where it accompanies bolognese sauce (rather than spaghetti). Fettuccine is the Roman version of tagliatelle and is cut slightly thinner.

Short Pasta

There are two types of short pasta: 'secca' is factory-made from durum wheat and water and 'pasta all'uovo' is made with eggs. There are numerous different shapes and some of the most popular ones are listed below.

Conchiglie Pasta shapes resembling conch shells. Sizes vary from tiny to large. They may be smooth or ridged conchiglie rigate.

Eliche and fusilli These are twisted into the shape of a screw.

Farfalle Bow or butterfly shaped, often with crinkled edges.

Macaroni Known as elbow macaroni or maccheroni in Italy. A thin, quick-cook variety is also available.

Penne Slightly larger than macaroni, the ends of these hollow tubes are cut diagonally and are pointed like quills.

Pipe Curved, hollow pasta and often sold ridged as pipe rigate.

Rigatoni Substantial, chunky, tubular pasta and often used for baking.

Rotelle Thin, wheel-shaped pasta, often sold in packets of two or three colours.

Stuffed Pasta

Tortellini The most common variety, consisting of tiny, stuffed pieces of pasta. Larger ones are called tortelloni. Cappelletti, ravioli and agnalotti are sometimes sold dried, but are often available fresh.

Fresh Pasta

Fresh pasta can be found in supermarkets and specialist shops. It is generally available in the same shapes as dried pasta.

How to Cook Perfect Pasta

Follow a few simple rules to ensure that your pasta is cooked to perfection every time:

1 Choose a large saucepan – there needs to be plenty of room for the pasta to move around so it does not stick together.

2 Cook the pasta in a large quantity of fast-boiling, well-salted water; ideally 4 litres/7 pints water and 1½–2 tablespoons of salt for every 350–450 g/12 oz–1 lb of pasta.

3 Tip in the pasta all at once, stir and cover. Return to a rolling boil, then remove the lid. Once it is boiling, lower the heat to medium-high and cook the pasta for the required time. It should be 'al dente' or tender, but still firm to the bite.

4 Drain, reserving a little of the cooking water to stir into the pasta. This helps to thin the sauce, if necessary, and helps prevent the pasta sticking together as it cools.

Serving Quantities

As an approximate guide, allow 75–100 g (3–4 oz) uncooked pasta per person. The amount will depend on whether the pasta is being served for a light or main meal and the type of sauce that it is being served with.

Rice

Varieties

Rice is the staple food of many countries throughout the world. Every country and culture has its own repertoire of rice recipes – India, for example, has the aromatic biryani, Spain has the saffron-scented paella, and Italy has the creamy risotto. Rice is grown on marshy, flooded land where other cereals cannot thrive and because it is grown in so many different areas, there is a huge range of rice types.

Long-grain white rice Probably the most widely used type of rice. Long-grain white rice has been milled so that the husk, bran and germ is removed. Easy-cook long-grain white rice has been steamed under pressure before milling. Pre-cooked rice, also known as par-boiled or converted rice, is polished white rice which is half-cooked after milling, then dried again. It is quick to cook but has a bland flavour.

Long-grain brown rice Where the outer husk is removed, leaving the bran and germ behind. This retains more of the fibre, vitamins and minerals. It has a nutty, slightly chewy texture and takes longer to cook than white rice.

Basmati rice This slender long-grain rice, which may be white or brown, is grown in the foothills of the Himalayas. After harvesting, it is allowed to mature for a year, giving it a unique aromatic flavour, hence its name, which means fragrant.

Risotto rice Grown in the north of Italy, this is the only rice that is suitable for making risotto. The grains are plump and have the ability to absorb large quantities of liquid without becoming too soft, cooking to a creamy texture with a slight bite. There are two grades of risotto rice: superfino and fino. Arborio rice is the most widely sold variety of the former, but you may also find carnaroli, Roma and baldo. Fino rice such as vialone nano has a slightly shorter grain, but the flavour is still excellent.

Valencia rice Traditionally used for Spanish paella, Valencia rice is soft and tender when ready. The medium-sized grains break down easily, so should be left unstirred during cooking to absorb the flavour of the stock and other ingredients.

Jasmine rice Also known as Thai fragrant rice, this long-grain rice has a delicate, almost perfumed aroma and flavour and has a soft, sticky texture.

Japanese sushi rice This is similar to glutinous rice in that it has a sticky texture. When mixed with rice vinegar it is easy to roll up with a filling inside to make sushi.

Pudding rice This rounded, short-grain rice is ideal for rice desserts. The grains swell and absorb large quantities of milk during cooking, giving puddings a rich, creamy consistency.

Wild rice This is an aquatic grass grown in North America rather than a true variety of rice. The black grains are long and slender and after harvesting and cleaning they are toasted to remove the chaff and intensify the nutty flavour and slight chewiness. It is often sold as a mixture with long-grain rice.

Rice flour Raw rice can be finely ground to make rice flour, which may be used to thicken sauces (1 tablespoon will thicken 300 ml/$\frac{1}{2}$ pint of liquid) or in Asian desserts. It is also used to make rice noodles.

Buying and Storing Rice

Rice will keep for several years if kept in sealed packets. However, it is at its best when fresh. To ensure freshness, always buy rice from reputable shops with a good turnover and buy in small quantities. Once opened, store the rice in an airtight container in a cool, dry place to keep out moisture. Most rice (but not risotto) benefits from washing before cooking – tip into a sieve and rinse under cold running water until the water runs clear. This removes any starch still clinging to the grains. Cooked rice will keep for up to two days if cooled and stored in a covered bowl in the refrigerator. If eating rice cold, serve within 24 hours – after this time it should be thoroughly re-heated.

Cooking Techniques

There are countless ways to cook rice, but much depends on the variety of rice being used, the dish being prepared and the desired results. Each variety of rice has its own characteristics. Some types of rice cook to light, separate grains, some to a rich, creamy consistency and some to a consistency where the grains stick together. Different types of rice have different powers of absorption. Long-grain rice will absorb three times its weight in water, whereas 25 g/1 oz of short-grain pudding rice can soak up a massive 300 ml/½ pint of liquid.

Cooking Long-grain Rice

The simplest method of cooking long-grain rice is to add it to plenty of boiling, salted water in a large saucepan. Allow 50 g/2 oz of rice per person when cooking as an accompaniment. Rinse under cold running water until clear then tip into rapidly boiling water. Stir once, then when the water returns to the boil, reduce the heat and simmer uncovered. Allow 10–12 minutes for white rice and 30–40 minutes for brown – check the packet for specific timings. The easiest way to test if rice is cooked is to bite a couple of grains – they should be tender but still firm. Drain immediately, then return to the pan with a little butter and herbs if liked. Fluff up with a fork and serve. To keep the rice warm, put it in a bowl and place over a pan of barely simmering water. Cover the top of the bowl with a tea towel until ready to serve.

Absorption Method

Cooking rice using the absorption method is also simple. Weigh out the quantity, then measure it by volume in a measuring jug – you will need 150 ml/¼ pint for two people. Rinse the rice then tip into a large saucepan. If liked, cook the rice in a little butter or oil for 1 minute. Pour in two parts water or stock to one part rice, season with salt and bring to the boil. Cover, then simmer gently until the liquid is absorbed and the rice is tender. White rice will take 15 minutes to cook, whereas brown rice will take 35 minutes. If there is still a little liquid left when the rice is tender, uncover and cook for 1 minute until evaporated. Remove from the heat and leave, covered, for 4–5 minutes then fluff up before serving. This method is good for cooking Jasmine and Valencia rice.

Oven-Baked Method

The oven-baked method also works by absorption, but takes longer than cooking on the hob. To make

oven-baked rice for two people, fry a chopped onion in 1 tablespoon olive oil in a 1.1 litre/2 pint flameproof casserole dish until soft and golden. Add 75 g/3 oz long-grain rice and cook for 1 minute, then stir in 300 ml/½ pint of stock – add a finely pared strip of lemon rind or bay leaf if liked. Cover and bake in a preheated oven at 180°C/350°F/Gas Mark 4 for 40 minutes, or until the rice is tender and all the stock has been absorbed. Fluff up before serving.

Cooking in the Microwave

Place rinsed long-grain rice in a large, heatproof bowl. Add boiling water or stock, allowing 300 ml/½ pint for 100 g/4 oz rice and 550 ml/18 fl oz for 225 g/8 oz rice. Add a pinch of salt and a knob of butter, if desired. Cover with clingfilm which has been pierced and cook on high for 3 minutes. Stir, re-cover and cook on medium for 12 minutes for white rice and 25 minutes for brown. Leave, covered, for 5 minutes before fluffing up and serving.

In a Pressure Cooker

Follow the quantities given for the absorption method and bring to the boil in the pressure cooker. Stir, cover and bring to a high 6.8 kg/15 lb pressure. Lower the heat and cook for 5 minutes if white rice or for 8 minutes for brown.

In a Rice Cooker

Follow the quantities given for the absorption method. Put the rice, salt and boiling water or stock in the cooker, return to the boil and cover. When all the liquid has been absorbed the cooker will turn off automatically.

Health and Nutrition

Rice is low in fat and high in complex carbohydrates, which are absorbed slowly and help to maintain blood sugar levels. It is also a reasonable source of protein and provides many B vitamins and the minerals potassium and phosphorus. It is a gluten-free cereal, making it suitable for coeliacs. Brown rice is richer in nutrients and fibre than refined white rice.

Herbs & Spices

In a culture where fast food, ready-made meals and processed foods are popular, homemade food can sometimes taste bland by comparison, due to the fact that the palate can quickly become accustomed to additives and flavour enhancers. The use of herbs and spices, however, can make all the difference in helping to make delicious homemade dishes.

Herbs are easy to grow and a garden is not needed as they can easily thrive on a small patio, window box or even on a windowsill. It is worth the effort to plant a few herbs as they do not require much attention or nurturing. The reward will be a range of fresh herbs available whenever needed and fresh flavours which cannot be beaten to add to any dish that is being prepared. While fresh herbs should be picked or bought as close as possible to the time of use, freeze-dried and dried herbs and spices will usually keep for around six months. The best idea is to buy little and often, and to store the herbs in airtight jars in a cool, dark cupboard. Fresh herbs tend to have a milder flavour than dried and equate to around one level tablespoon of fresh to one level teaspoon of dried. As a result, quantities used in cooking should be altered accordingly. A variety of herbs and spices and their uses are listed below.

Allspice The dark allspice berries come whole or ground and have a flavour similar to that of cinnamon, cloves and nutmeg. Although not the same as mixed spices, allspice can be used with pickles, relishes, cakes and milk puddings, or whole in meat and fish dishes.

Aniseed Comes in whole seeds or ground. It has a strong aroma and flavour and should be used sparingly in baking and salad dressings.

Basil Best fresh but also available in dried form, basil can be used raw or cooked and works well in many dishes but is particularly well-suited to tomato-based dishes and sauces, salads and Mediterranean dishes.

Bay leaves Available in fresh or dried form as well as ground. They make up part of a bouquet garni and are particularly delicious when added to meat and poultry dishes, soups, stews, vegetable dishes and stuffing. They also impart a spicy flavour to milk puddings and egg custards.

Caraway seeds These have a warm, sweet taste and are often used in breads and cakes, but are also delicious with cabbage dishes and pickles.

Cayenne The powdered form of a red chilli pepper said to be native to Cayenne. It is similar in appearance to paprika and can be used sparingly to add a fiery kick to many dishes.

Cardamom Has a distinctive sweet, rich taste and can be bought whole in the pod, in seed form or ground. This sweet aromatic spice is delicious in curries, rice, cakes and biscuits and is great served with rice pudding and fruit.

Chervil Reminiscent of parsley and available either in fresh or dried form, chervil has a faintly sweet, spicy flavour and is particularly good in soups, cheese dishes, stews and with eggs.

Chilli Available whole, fresh, dried and in powdered form, red chillies tend to be sweeter in taste than their green counterparts. They are particularly associated with Spanish and Mexican-style cooking and curries, but are also delicious with pickles, dips, sauces and in pizza toppings.

Chives Best used when fresh but also available in dried form, this member of the onion family is ideal for use when a delicate onion flavour is required. Chives are good with eggs, cheese, fish and vegetable dishes. They also work well as a garnish for soups, meat and vegetable dishes.

Cinnamon Comes in the form of reddish-brown sticks of bark from an evergreen tree and has a sweet pungent aroma. Either whole or ground, cinnamon is delicious in cakes and milk puddings, particularly with apple, and is used in mulled wine and for preserving.

Cloves Mainly used whole although available ground, cloves have a very warm, sweet, pungent aroma and can be used to stud roast ham and pork, in mulled wine and punch and when pickling fruit. When ground, they can be used in making mincemeat and in Christmas puddings and biscuits.

Coriander Coriander seeds have an orangey flavour and are available whole or ground. Coriander is particularly delicious (whether whole or roughly ground) in casseroles, curries and as a pickling spice. The leaves are used both to flavour spicy aromatic dishes as well as a garnish.

Cumin Also available ground or as whole seeds, cumin has a strong, slightly bitter flavour. It is one of the main ingredients in curry powder and compliments many fish, meat and rice dishes.

Dill These leaves are available fresh or dried and have a mild flavour, while the seeds are slightly bitter. Dill is particularly good with salmon, new potatoes and in sauces. The seeds are good in pickles and vegetable dishes.

Fennel Whole seeds or ground, fennel has a fragrant, sweet aniseed flavour and is sometimes known as the fish herb because it compliments fish dishes so well.

Ginger Comes in many forms but primarily as a fresh root and in dried, ground form, which can be used in baking, curries, pickles, sauces and Chinese cooking.

Lemon grass Available fresh and dried, with a subtle, aromatic, lemony flavour, lemon grass is essential to Thai cooking. It is also delicious when added to soups, poultry and fish dishes.

Mace The outer husk of nutmeg has a milder nutmeg flavour and can be used in pickles, cheese dishes, stewed fruits, sauces and hot punch.

Marjoram Often dried, marjoram has a sweet, slightly spicy flavour, which tastes fantastic when added to stuffing, meat or tomato-based dishes.

Mint Available fresh or dried, mint has a strong, sweet aroma which is delicious in a sauce or jelly to serve with lamb. It is also great with fresh peas and new potatoes and is an essential ingredient in Pimms.

Nutmeg The large, whole seeds have a warm, sweet taste and compliment custards, milk puddings, cheese dishes, parsnips and creamy soups.

Oregano These strongly flavoured dried leaves are similar to marjoram and are used extensively in Italian and Greek cooking.

Paprika Often comes in two varieties. One is quite sweet and mild and the other has a slight bite to it. Paprika is made from the fruit of the sweet pepper and is good in meat and poultry dishes as well as a garnish. The rule of buying herbs and spices little and often applies particularly to paprika as unfortunately it does not keep particularly well.

Parsley The stems as well as the leaves of parsley can be used to compliment most savoury dishes as they contain the most flavour. They can also be used as a garnish.

Poppy seeds These small, grey-black coloured seeds impart a sweet, nutty flavour when added to biscuits, vegetable dishes, dressings and cheese dishes.

Rosemary Delicious fresh or dried, these small, needle-like leaves have a sweet aroma which is particularly good with lamb, stuffing and vegetables dishes. Also delicious when added to charcoal on the barbecue to give a piquant flavour to meat and corn on the cob.

Saffron Deep orange in colour, saffron is traditionally used in paella, rice and cakes but is also delicious with poultry. Saffron is the most expensive of all spices.

Sage These fresh or dried leaves have a pungent, slightly bitter taste which is delicious with pork and poultry, sausages, stuffing and with stuffed pasta when tossed in a little butter and fresh sage.

Sesame Sesame seeds have a nutty taste, especially when toasted, and are delicious in baking, on salads, or with Far-Eastern cooking.

Tarragon The fresh or dried leaves of tarragon have a sweet aromatic taste, which is particularly good with poultry, seafood, fish, creamy sauces and stuffing.

Thyme Available fresh or dried, thyme has a pungent flavour and is included in bouquet garni. It compliments many meat and poultry dishes and stuffing.

Turmeric Obtained from the root of a lily from southeast Asia. This root is ground and has a brilliant yellow colour. It has a bitter, peppery flavour and is often combined for use in curry powder and mustard. Also delicious in pickles, relishes and dressings.

Entertaining

There are many ways of entertaining friends and family, and whether it is an informal or formal occasion, there are some rules that can be applied to all entertaining that will help make life easy for the host and hostess.

First of all, decide what kind of entertaining you wish to do: dinner party, supper, barbecue, picnic, cheese and wine or even a disco. This will dictate how formal the event will be, These days parties tend to be far more informal and relaxed, but even so it is still advisable to be guided by a few rules.

Make Life Easy

- Decide how many guests to invite and check their dietary requirements – are they vegetarian, do they have allergies to certain foods or have specific likes or dislikes?
- Choose the venue and menu and decide on the drinks to serve, ensuring that there are plenty of soft drinks for those driving.
- Make a shopping list ahead of time. This will allow for non-perishable foods to be bought early, as well as leaving time for a change of menu if necessary.
- Check china, cutlery, glasses and table linen. Make sure that it is clean and you have sufficient for all the guests.
- If it helps, work out a time plan early on. This will enable you to cook ahead if possible, thus saving time and effort on the day.
- If trying a new recipe, it is advisable to cook it beforehand to ensure that it works and tastes good.
- Arrange flowers the day before. Ensure you have nibbles and appetisers to serve, and stock up on ice, mixer drinks, lemon and glasses. Make sure you have plenty of coffee, tea or other after-dinner drinks.

Menu Planning for Different Occasions

Drinks Parties

These are normally semi-informal, and unless you serve very expensive wines or champagne, relatively cheap. Although food is not served as at an actual meal, it is a good idea to serve some light starters. This will help to offset too much alcoholic drink. People tend to eat more than you might think and it is a good idea to offer at least four or five different snacks as well as the obligatory nuts, crisps and little biscuits. Try to offer at least two vegetarian choices.

Try serving bite-sized vol-au-vents, perhaps filled with peeled prawns in a flavoured mayonnaise or chicken and sweetcorn. Small squares of quiche are good, or try roasted peppers with blue cheese.

more than three, ensure that all the courses compliment each other and that the portions are not too large. Invite guests to arrive at least 30 minutes before you hope to sit down – this allows for guests arriving late.

Menus should be balanced: normally the dinner should start with a soup or small appetiser, and fish can be served either as the main course or as a second course as a prelude to the meat or poultry. Cheese and dessert are served after the main course; it is a matter of personal preference which is served first.

Supper, Lunch or Brunch Parties

These are normally much more informal and spur-of-the-moment events. However, a little planning is an excellent idea so that the host or hostess does not spend the entire time dashing around, making both themselves and the guests stressed trying to ensure that everyone enjoys the occasion.

Obviously, the menu will depend on the time of year and the ages of those involved. Younger people are more than happy with fast food such as pizza or baked chicken pieces, with plenty of crisps and oven baked chips or a large bowl of pasta. Try a theme for your party such as Italian or Oriental. There are many excellent Chinese and pasta dishes in this book to choose from.

Smoked salmon and asparagus rolls, in both white and brown bread, cocktail sausages on sticks with a sweet chilli dip and chicken satay on sticks with satay sauces are all fairly straightforward. Hand round either small napkins or plates so guests can take a few at a time and do not spill the food on themselves or your furniture.

Keep drinks simple – do not offer everything. People are quite happy with a limited choice, red or white wine and beer with plenty of soft drinks is perfectly acceptable, or in winter try a warming punch. Pimms in the summer is an ideal choice.

Formal Dinner Party

These take a little more planning, both in terms of which guests to invite and the food. When working out the invitations, ensure that all your guests will get on well together and that there is at least one thing they have in common. Always remember to check their dietary requirements. Dinner parties can consist of as many courses as wished. If offering

Barbecue Parties

In this county, because of the weather, barbecues have to be fairly impromptu, meaning that the food needs to be simple and adaptable. Depending on tastes, keep the food quick and easy to prepare – the best choices are steak, chicken pieces, small whole fish such as sardines, and sausages, all of which can be cooked whole or cut into cubes and skewered and marinated to make kebabs. These cook quickly and will be ready in a very short time. Serve plenty of salads and bread. If cooking chicken portions which still contain the bones, it is advisable to cook them in the oven first and finish them on the barbecue to ensure that the chicken is thoroughly cooked through.

When barbecuing, it is vital that the food is cooked properly. If using a barbecue that uses coal, light it in plenty of time (at least 20 minutes before required) to allow the coals to reach the correct temperature before commencing to cook. The coals should be white/grey in colour and coated in ash, and the flames should have died down to give a good, steady heat.

Eating outside often sharpens the appetite, so along with the meats serve plenty of bread or potatoes with assorted salads. Coleslaw and rice and pasta salads all work well. Keep desserts and drinks simple: fresh fruit, ice cream or cheese with wine or beer to drink.

Children's Parties

The highlight of any child's year is their birthday party, and to avoid tears, a little planning is a good idea. Many companies now offer a complete service so that the children can participate in an activity, such as skating, football or swimming, then the birthday tea is provided and all that is expected of the parents is to take and collect. This is by far one of the easiest and least stressful ways to celebrate their day, but can be expensive.

If that is not for you, above all keep it simple, whether you hold the party at home or in a local hall. First, decide on a date and venue and how long the party will be. Send out the invitations in plenty of time, stating clearly what time it will finish – most important for your sanity. Enlist the help of at least two other adults who are used to dealing with tears and tantrums. Decide on a few games, depending on age, such as pass the parcel, pin the tail on the donkey, musical chairs or blind man's bluff. Clear away furniture and any breakable ornaments and ensure that no sharp objects are in easy reach of little fingers.

Serve the food in a separate room and keep it fairly plain. Too much rich food could result in a few children being ill. Go for simple sandwiches, small pieces of cheese with grapes, sausages, sausage rolls, crisps, fairy cakes and, of course, a birthday cake. Serve squash to drink.

Many parties finish with the guests being issued with a goody bag to take home. If you do this, keep it simple: a few sweets, a piece of birthday cake and two or three very small gifts is perfectly acceptable. There is no need to spend a lot on these.

Wines

There are many different and excellent wines to choose from: white, red or rosé, sweet, medium or dry coming from all parts of the world. When choosing wines for a special occasion there are few points to bear in mind.

- Work out how many bottles you require. Allow 5–6 glasses from each bottle of wine; for fortified wines, sherry, Madeira and port allow 12–16 glasses. Champagne also yields between 5–6 glasses.
- Choose wines that are of medium price. Cheap wines taste cheap and your guests will not be impressed; expensive wines, on the other hand, will most probably not be appreciated in the general chat and movement.
- White wine is best served chilled. Place in the refrigerator at least the day before. If space is short, arrange for some ice for the day, place in a wine bucket or any clean container and chill the wine in this.
- Red wine should be served at room temperature, so if stored in a cool place, bring into another room and allow to come to room temperature. Open about 1–2 hours before serving. There is no need to decant either white or red wine, but it does look good and also allows red wine to breathe more easily. For wine with a heavy sediment it is advisable to decant it.
- For the greatest appreciation, red wine glasses should be wide-necked, allowing the bouquet to be enjoyed. White wine glasses are narrow at the neck.
  All should have a stem so that the glasses can be swirled in order to release the fragrance.

Know Your Wine

France

Renowned for its fine wines, Champagnes and excellent table wines. The Appellations d'Origines Contrôlées (A.O.C.) is a system that signifies if a wine comes from a fine wine region. Indicating different grades of quality, these appellations go in stages from simple wines to prized wines such as Beaune, Chateau Neuf du Pape and Sancerre. Simple vins des tables are blended wines that generally offer excellent value for money.

Germany

German wines have improved considerably over the last 40 years. Gone, in the main, are the sweet white wines and heavy, rough reds. In their place are delicate, crisp wines from the Moselle and Rhine using the Riesling grape, and others such as Traminer, Sylvaner and other varieties blended together. Hock is perhaps one of the most well-known wines and comes from the four main regions in the Rhine. There are many fine wines, which carry the name of the grape.

Italy

Most of the regions of Italy produce wine, as do Sardinia and Sicily. When buying Italian wines, look for D.O.C. on the label. They produce both white and red, perhaps the most well-known of which is Chianti. This wine comes from Tuscany and is a fruity and robust wine and goes well with all red meats and game. Other red wines include Barolo from Piedmont and Valpolicella from the Veneto region. There are other excellent red wines from the north made from the Cabernet, Pinot and Merlot grapes. Italy also produces some excellent white wines, ranging from Soave, Verdicchio, Frascati and Pinot Grigio – all have their own distinct style ranging from very dry, light wine to a heavier, sweeter wine.

Spain

Although Spain is world-famous for sherry, it also produces some excellent wines. The best-known is probably Rioja, which is produced both as white and red. This wine is produced throughout the whole of Spain, with the red Rioja coming in two styles, one being drier than the other, and the white tending to be full-bodied and dry.

New World

There are now some serious contenders to 'Old World' wines coming from as far afield as Australia – known as a 'New World' wine producer. Australia, South Africa, Chile and California all produce excellent wines that seriously challenge the established wine-growers. Growers from these countries have taken on-board all the established guidelines and knowledge and have expanded it to produce wines that are every bit as good. When buying New World wine, apply the same guidelines as for the established wines.

Useful Conversions

Liquid Measures
Metric/Imperial

2.5 ml	½ teaspoon	900 ml	1½ pints
5 ml	1 teaspoon	1 litre	1¾ pints
15 ml	1 tablespoon	1.2 litres	2 pints
25 ml	1 fl oz	1.25 litres	2¼ pints
50 ml	2 fl oz	1.5 litres	2½ pints
65 ml	2½ fl oz	1.6 litres	2¾ pints
85 ml	3 fl oz	1.7 litres	3 pints
100 ml	3½ fl oz	2 litres	3½ pints
120 ml	4 fl oz	2.25 litres	4 pints
135 ml	4½ fl oz	2.5 litres	4½ pints
150 ml	¼ pint (5 fl oz) 8 tablespoons	2.75 litres	5 pints
175 ml	6 fl oz		
200 ml	7 fl oz (⅓ pint)		
250 ml	8 fl oz		
275 ml	9 fl oz		
300 ml	½ pint (10 fl oz)		
350 ml	12 fl oz		
400 ml	14 fl oz		
450 ml	¾ pint (15 fl oz)		
475 ml	16 fl oz		
500 ml	18 fl oz		
600 ml	1 pint (20 fl oz)		
750 ml	1¼ pints		

Temperature Conversion

−4°F	−20°C	68°F	20°C
5°F	−15°C	77°F	25°C
14°F	−10°C	86°F	30°C
23°F	−5°C	95°F	35°C
32°F	0°C	104°F	40°C
41°F	5°C	113°F	45°C
50°F	10°C	122°F	50°C
59°F	15°C	212°F	100°C

Dry Weights
Metric/Imperial

10 g	¼ oz	165 g	5½ oz	450 g	1 lb (16 oz)
15 g	½ oz	175 g	6 oz		
20 g	¾ oz	185 g	6½ oz		
25 g	1 oz	200 g	7 oz		
40 g	1½ oz	225 g	8 oz		
50 g	2 oz	250 g	9 oz		
65 g	2½ oz	300 g	10 oz		
75 g	3 oz	325 g	11 oz		
90 g	3½ oz	350 g	12 oz		
100 g	4 oz	375 g	13 oz		
120 g	4½ oz	400 g	14 oz		
150 g	5 oz	425 g	15 oz		

Oven Temperatures

110°C	225°F	Gas Mark ¼	Very slow oven
120/130°C	250°F	Gas Mark ½	Very slow oven
140°C	275°F	Gas Mark 1	Slow oven
150°C	300°F	Gas Mark 2	Slow oven
160/170°C	325°F	Gas Mark 3	Moderate oven
180°C	350°F	Gas Mark 4	Moderate oven
190°C	375°F	Gas Mark 5	Moderately hot oven
200°C	400°F	Gas Mark 6	Moderately hot oven
220°C	425°F	Gas Mark 7	Hot oven
230°C	450°F	Gas Mark 8	Hot oven
240°C	475°F	Gas Mark 9	Very hot oven

Good Cooking Rules

When handling and cooking foods, there are a few rules and guidelines that should be observed so that food remains fit to eat and uncontaminated with the bacteria and bugs that can result in food poisoning.

Good Hygiene Rules

- Personal hygiene is imperative when handling food. Before commencing any preparation, wash hands thoroughly with soap, taking particular care with nails. Always wash hands after going to the toilet. Wash again after handling raw foods, cooked meats or vegetables. Do not touch any part of the body or handle pets, rubbish or dirty washing during food preparation.
- Cuts should be covered with a waterproof plaster, preferably blue so it can be easily seen if lost.
- Do not smoke in the kitchen.
- Keep pets off all work surfaces and out of the kitchen if possible. Clean surfaces with an anti-bacterial solution. Wash their eating bowls separately.
- Ensure that hair is off the face and does not trail into food or machinery.
- Use a dishwasher wherever possible and wash utensils and equipment in the very hot, soapy water.
- Use clean dish cloths and tea towels, replacing regularly. Boil them to kill any bacteria, and use absorbent kitchen paper where possible to wipe hands and equipment.
- Chopping boards and cooking implements must be clean. Boards should either be washed in a dishwasher or scrubbed after each use. Keep a separate board for meat, fish and vegetables and wash knives before using on different types of food. Do not use the same board for raw and cooked food: wash in-between, or better still, use a different board.
- Use dustbin liners for rubbish and empty regularly, cleaning your bin with disinfectant. Dustbins should be outside.

Guidelines for Using a Refrigerator

- Ensure that the refrigerator is situated away from any equipment that gives off heat, such as the cooker, washing machine or tumble drier, to ensures the greatest efficiency. Ensure that the vents are not obstructed.
- If not frost-free, defrost regularly, wiping down with a mild solution of bicarbonate of soda dissolved in warm water and a clean cloth.
- Close the door as quickly as possible so that the motor does not have to work overtime to keep it at the correct temperature.
- Ensure that the temperature is 5°C. A thermometer is a good investment.
- Avoid over-loading – this just makes the motor work harder.
- Cool food before placing in the refrigerator and always cover to avoid any smells or transference of taste to other foods.

Stacking Your Refrigerator

- Remove supermarket packaging from raw meat, poultry and fish, place on a plate or dish, cover loosely and store at the base of the refrigerator to ensure that the juices do not drip on other foods.
- Store cheese in a box or container, wrapped to prevent the cheese drying out.
- Remove food to be eaten raw 30 minutes before use so it can return to room temperature.
- Cooked meats, bacon and all cooked dishes should be stored at the top – this is the coldest part.
- Store eggs in the egg compartment and remove 30 minutes before cooking in order to return them to temperature.
- Butter and all fats can be stored on the door, as can milk, cold drinks, sauces, mayonnaise and preserves with low sugar content.
- Cream and other dairy products, as well as pastries such as chocolate éclairs, should be stored on the middle shelf.
- Vegetables, salad and fruit should be stored in the salad boxes at the bottom of the refrigerator.
- Soft fruits should be kept in the salad box along with mushrooms, which are best kept in paper bags.
- To avoid cross-contamination, raw and cooked foods must be stored separately.
- Use all foods by the sell-by date – once opened, treat as cooked foods and use within two days.

General Rules

- Use all foods by the use-by date and store correctly. This applies to all foods: fresh, frozen, canned and dried. Potatoes are best if removed from polythene, stored in brown paper and kept in the cool and dark.
- Ensure that all food is thoroughly thawed before use, unless meant to be cooked from frozen.
- Cook all poultry thoroughly at the correct temperature (190°C/375°F/Gas Mark 5) ensuring that the juices run clear.
- Leave foods to cool as quickly as possible before placing in the refrigerator, and cover while cooling.
- Do not re-freeze any thawed frozen foods unless cooked first.
- Date and label frozen food and use in rotation.
- Re-heat foods thoroughly until piping hot. Remember to allow foods to stand when using the microwave and stir to distribute the heat.
- Microwaves vary according to make and wattage – always refer to manufacturer's instructions.
- Only re-heat dishes once and always heat until piping hot.
- Ensure that eggs are fresh. If using for mayonnaise, soufflés or other dishes that use raw or semi-cooked egg, do not give to the vulnerable – the elderly, pregnant women, those with a recurring illness, toddlers and babies.
- When buying frozen foods, transport in freezer-insulated bags, placing in the freezer as soon as possible after purchase.
- Chilled foods, such as cold meats, cheese, fresh meat, fish and dairy products should be bought, taken home and placed in the refrigerator immediately. Do not keep in a warm car or room.
- Avoid buying damaged or unlabelled canned goods. Keep store cupboards clean, wiping down regularly and rotating the food.
- Flour, nuts, rice, pulses, grains and pasta should be checked regularly and once opened, placed in airtight containers.
- Do not buy eggs or frozen or chilled foods that are damaged in any way.
- Keep dried herbs and ready-ground spices in a cool, dark place, not in a spice rack on the work surface. They quickly lose their pungency and flavour when exposed to light.

Basic Recipes

Once you have mastered these simple but essential recipes for eggs, pastry, vegetables, fish, meat and sweet dishes you will be ready to attempt anything. Your introduction to cookery begins here.

Eggs

Boiled Eggs

Eggs should be boiled in gently simmering water. Remove the egg from the refrigerator at least 30 minutes before cooking. Bring a pan of water to the boil, then once boiling lower the heat to a simmer. Gently lower the egg into the water and cook for 3 minutes for lightly set, or 4 minutes for a slightly firmer set. Remove and lightly tap to stop the egg continuing to cook. Hard boiled eggs should be cooked for 10 minutes then plunged into cold water and left until cold before shelling. Serve lightly boiled eggs with toast or buttered bread cut into fingers to use as dippers.

Fried Eggs

Place a little sunflower oil or butter in a frying pan until hot. Break an egg into a cup or small jug and carefully slip into the pan. Cook, spooning the hot oil or fat over the egg for 3–4 minutes or until set to personal preference. Remove with a palette knife or fish slice

and serve with freshly grilled bacon or sausages or on fried bread with baked beans and tomatoes.

Poached Eggs

Half-fill a frying pan with water and bring to a gentle boil, then reduce the heat to a simmer. Add either a little salt or a few drops of vinegar or lemon juice – this will help the egg retain its shape. Break the egg into a cup or small jug and carefully slip into the simmering water. Lightly oiled round, plain pastry cutters can be used to contain the eggs if preferred. Cover the pan with a lid and cook for 3–4 minutes or until set to personal preference. Once cooked, remove by draining with a slotted draining spoon or fish slice and serve. Alternatively, special poaching pans are available if preferred. With these, half-fill the pan with water and place the tray with the egg containers on top. Place a little butter in the cups and bring to the boil. Swirl the melted butter around and carefully slip in the

eggs. Cover with the lid and cook for 3–4 minutes. Serve either on hot buttered toast or on top of sliced ham or freshly cooked spinach.

Scrambled Eggs

Melt 15 g/½ oz butter in a small pan. Allowing two eggs per person, break the eggs into a small bowl and add 1 tablespoon of milk and seasoning to taste. Whisk until blended with a fork, then pour into the melted butter. Cook over a gentle heat, stirring with a wooden spoon, until set and creamy. Serve on hot buttered toast with smoked salmon or stir in some freshly snipped chives or chopped tomatoes.

Omelette

Allow two eggs per person. Break the eggs into a small bowl, add seasoning to taste and 1 tablespoon of milk. Whisk with a fork until frothy. Heat 2 teaspoons of olive oil in a frying pan, and, when hot, pour in the egg mixture. Cook gently, stirring with the fork, and bringing the mixture from the edges of the pan to the centre. Allow the uncooked egg mixture to flow to the edges. When the egg has set, cook without stirring for an extra minute before folding the omelette into three and gently turning out onto a warmed serving plate. Take care not to overcook.

Cheese Omelette

Proceed as before, then sprinkle 25–40 g/1–1 ½ oz grated mature Cheddar cheese on top of the lightly set omelette. Cook for a further 2 minutes or until the cheese has begun to melt. If liked, place under a preheated grill for 2–3 minutes or until golden, fold over and serve.

Tomato Omelette

Proceed as for a plain omelette and after 2 minutes of cooking time, add 1 medium chopped tomato on top of the omelette and cook as above until set.

Fine Herbs Omelette

Stir in 1 tablespoon of finely chopped, fresh mixed herbs into the beaten eggs before cooking. Proceed as for a plain omelette.

Mushroom Omelette

Wipe and slice 50 g/2 oz button mushrooms. Heat 15 g/½ oz of butter in a small pan and cook the mushrooms for 2–3 minutes, drain and reserve. Cook omelette as above, adding the cooked mushrooms once it is lightly set.

Vegetables

Blanched Vegetables

Vegetables are often blanched to preserve their colour or to speed up the cooking process. This technique is normally used for green vegetables and peppers. Trim or peel the vegetable, according to each variety, and cut into small pieces or as directed in the recipe. Rinse well. Bring a pan of lightly salted water to the boil, add the vegetables, cover with a lid, reduce the heat and simmer for 2–4 minutes or as directed. Remove, drain and plunge the vegetables immediately into cold water. Leave until cold, then drain and use.

Blanched Chips

Peel some even-sized potatoes and cut into either thin or chunky chips as desired. Cover in cold water and soak for at least 10 minutes to remove the starch, then drain thoroughly and dry on a clean tea towel. Cover a chip basket with a layer of chips, and heat a deep-fat fryer half-filled with oil to a temperature of 180°C/350°F. Plunge the chips into the oil and cook for 3–4 minutes or until soft but not coloured. Drain and place on a tray. Repeat with the remaining chips. When ready to fry, heat the oil to 190°C/375°F, arrange a layer of chips in the chip basket and carefully lower into the hot oil. Cook for 3–5 minutes or until crisp and golden. Drain on absorbent paper and repeat with the remaining chips.

Par-boiled Potatoes and Parsnips

Peel and trim the potatoes and parsnips, discarding any eyes or damaged vegetables. Cut into even-sized pieces. Place separately in large saucepans, add a little salt and cover with cold water. Bring to the boil, cover with lids, reduce the heat and simmer for 5 minutes. Drain, return the vegetables to the saucepans and cover with the lids. Heat gently for about 5 minutes, shaking the pans so as to slightly break up the surface of the vegetables. Use as required.

Roasted Potatoes

Par-boil potatoes as previously directed. For 450 g/ 1 lb potatoes, pour 1–2 tablespoons of sunflower or olive oil into a roasting tin and heat in a preheated hot oven at 200°C/400°F/Gas Mark 6 for 5–8 minutes or until really hot. Add the potatoes to the tin and turn in the hot oil. Cook for 50 minutes to 1 hour or until crisp and golden. Turn occasionally during roasting. Parsnips can be roasted in the same way and can, if liked, be cooked with the potatoes.

Roasted Vegetables

Clean, trim and peel the vegetables, discarding any seeds or stalks. Cut into even-sized pieces. Place in a roasting tin and pour over 2–3 tablespoons of olive oil. Peel and cut 2–3 garlic cloves into thick slices and scatter over the vegetables. Season to taste and add a few sprigs of fresh rosemary, thyme or oregano. Roast in a preheated oven at 200°C/400°F/Gas Mark 6 for 40–45 minutes or until tender and beginning to char around the edges. Turn occasionally during cooking. Vegetables suitable for roasting include onions, cut into wedges, assorted coloured peppers, courgettes, aubergines and carrots. Tomatoes and mushrooms will take less time to roast, about 20 minutes.

Frying Onions

Peel 450 g/1 lb onions, keeping the base of each onion intact (this will help to prevent 'crying' while peeling the onions). Heat 2–3 tablespoons of olive or sunflower oil in a large, heavy-based frying pan. Add the onions and sauté gently, stirring for 10–12 minutes or until the onions are soft but still retain a bite.

Caramelising Onions

Cook as above and after 10 minutes, sprinkle in 2 teaspoons of light muscovado sugar and continue to cook, stirring frequently for a further 10–15 minutes or until golden.

Sauces

White Pouring Sauce

Makes 300 ml/¹/₂ pt

15 g/¹/₂ oz butter or margarine

2 tbsp plain white flour

300 ml/¹/₂ pt milk

salt and freshly ground black pepper

Melt the butter or margarine in a small saucepan and stir in the flour. Cook, stirring over a gentle heat for 2 minutes, then draw off the heat and gradually stir in the milk. Return to the heat and cook, stirring with a wooden spoon until the sauce thickens and coats the back of the spoon. Add seasoning to taste and use as required.

For a coating sauce, use 25 g/1 oz of butter or margarine and 3 tablespoons of plain white flour to 300 ml/¹/₂ pt liquid and proceed as above.

For a binding sauce, use 50 g/2 oz butter or margarine and 50 g/2 oz plain white flour to 300 ml/¹/₂ pint liquid and proceed as above.

Cheese Sauce

Proceed as before, depending on which consistency is required, stirring in 1 tsp dried mustard powder with the flour. When the sauce has thickened, remove from the heat and stir in 50 g/2 oz mature Cheddar cheese, or any other cheese of choice. Stir until melted.

Herb Sauce

Make a white sauce as before, then stir in 1 tbsp freshly chopped herbs such as parsley, basil, oregano or a mixture of fresh herbs.

Mushroom Sauce

Make as before and lightly sauté 50 g/2 oz sliced mushrooms in 1 tablespoon of butter for 3 minutes or until tender. Drain and stir into the prepared white sauce.

Bechamel Sauce

Makes 300 ml/¹/₂ pint

Peel 1 small onion and place in a small saucepan together with a small piece of peeled carrot, a small celery stick, 3 whole cloves and a few black

peppercorns. Add 300 ml/½ pint milk and bring slowly to just below boiling point. Remove from the heat, cover with a lid and leave to infuse for at least 30 minutes. When ready to use, strain off the milk and use to make a white sauce as before. If liked, 1–2 tablespoons of single cream can be stirred in at the end of cooking.

Gravy
Makes 300 ml/½ pint
When roasting meat, once the meat is cooked, remove from the roasting tin, cover and keep warm. Pour off all but 2–3 tablespoons of the meat juices and heat on the hob. Stir in 2 tablespoons of plain

white flour and cook for 2 minutes, stirring the sediment that is left in the tin into the gravy. Draw off the heat and gradually stir in 300 ml/ ½ pint of stock, according to the flavour of the meat. Return to the heat and cook, stirring until the gravy comes to the boil and thickens. Add seasoning to taste and, if liked, a little port, wine or redcurrant jelly. Gravy browning can be added if desired to give a darker colour. If no meat juices are available, heat 2 tablespoons of oil and stir in 1–2 tablespoons of flour. Cook for 2 minutes then draw off the heat and stir in 300 ml/½ pint of stock of your choice. Return to the heat and cook, stirring until thickened. Add seasoning, flavourings and gravy browning according to personal preference.

Tomato Sauce
Makes 450 ml/¾ pint
1 tbsp olive or sunflower oil
1 small onion, peeled and finely chopped
1–2 garlic cloves, peeled and crushed
50 g/2 oz streaky bacon, optional
450 g/1 lb ripe tomatoes, peeled if preferred and chopped
  or 400 g can chopped tomatoes
1–2 tbsp tomato purée
150 ml/¼ pint vegetable stock
salt and freshly ground pepper
1 tbsp freshly chopped oregano, marjoram or basil

Heat the oil in a saucepan and sauté the onion, garlic and bacon, if using, for 5 minutes. Add the chopped tomatoes and sauté for a further 5 minutes, stirring

occasionally. Blend the tomato purée with the stock then pour into the pan, add seasoning and herbs and bring to the boil. Cover with a lid, reduce the heat and simmer for 12–15 minutes or until a chunky sauce is formed. Blend in a food processor to form a slightly less chunky sauce, or if a smoother sauce is preferred then rub through a fine sieve. Adjust seasoning and use as required.

Curry Sauce
Makes 300 ml/½ pint
1 tbsp sunflower oil
1 medium onion, peeled and chopped
2–4 garlic cloves, peeled and crushed
1 celery stick, trimmed and chopped
1–2 red chillies, deseeded and chopped
1 tsp ground coriander
1 tsp ground cumin
½ tsp turmeric
1 tbsp plain white flour
450 ml/¾ pt vegetable stock
salt and freshly ground black pepper
1 tbsp freshly chopped coriander, optional

Heat the oil in a saucepan and sauté the onion, garlic, celery and chillies for 5–8 minutes or until softened. Add the spices and continue to sauté for a further 3 minutes, stirring frequently. Sprinkle in the flour, cook for 2 minutes, then slowly add the stock and bring to the boil. Cover with a lid, reduce the heat and simmer for 15 minutes, stirring occasionally. Add seasoning to taste and stir in the chopped coriander if using. Use as required.

Apple Sauce
Makes 300 ml/¹/₂ pint
450 g/1 lb Bramley cooking apples, peeled,
  cored and chopped
1 tbsp butter
25–40 g/1¹/₂–2 oz sugar

Place all the ingredients with 2 tablespoons of water in a saucepan and cook over a gentle heat for 10 minutes, or until the apples are tender, stirring occasionally. Take care that the apples do not burn on the base of the pan. Remove from the heat and either rub through a sieve to form a smooth purée or beat with the spoon to give a chunkier sauce. The apple sauce can be flavoured with 1 tablespoon of finely grated orange or lemon rind and 2–3 whole cloves, which you should remove before serving. Alternatively, add 1 lightly bruised cinnamon stick (remove before serving).

Mint Sauce
Makes 120 ml/4 fl oz
15 g/¹/₂ oz fresh mint
1 tbsp caster sugar
3–4 tbsp white wine vinegar or other vinegar of choice

Discard the stalks from the mint, rinse the leaves and dry. Finely chop and place in a sauceboat or small bowl. Pour over 3–4 tablespoons of hot but not boiling water, then stir in the sugar until dissolved. Stir in the vinegar and use as required.

Cranberry Sauce
Makes 450 g/1 lb
450 g/1 lb fresh or thawed frozen cranberries
150 ml/¹/₄ pt orange juice
50 g/2 oz light muscovado sugar, or to taste
1–2 tbsp port, optional

Rinse the cranberries and place in a saucepan with the orange juice and sugar. Place over a gentle heat and cook, stirring occasionally for 12–15 minutes or until the cranberries are soft and have 'popped'. Remove from the heat and stir in the port, if using. Use as required.

Place the egg yolk in a bowl and stir in the mustard powder with a little seasoning and the sugar. Beat with a wooden spoon until blended then gradually add the oil, drop by drop, stirring briskly with either a whisk or wooden spoon. If the mixture becomes too thick, beat in a little of the vinegar or lemon juice. When all the oil has been added, stir in the remaining vinegar or lemon juice and adjust the seasoning. Store covered in the refrigerator until required.

If the mayonnaise should curdle whilst making, place a further egg in a separate bowl then slowly beat into the curdled mixture.

Tartare Sauce

Makes 150 ml/¹⁄₄ pint

150 ml/¹⁄₄ pt prepared mayonnaise

1 tbsp freshly chopped tarragon

1 tbsp freshly chopped parsley

1 tbsp capers, rinsed and chopped

1 tbsp gherkins, finely chopped

1 tbsp lemon juice

Mix all the ingredients together. Place in a small bowl, cover and leave for at least 30 minutes for the flavours to blend.

French Dressing

Makes 120 ml/4 fl oz

¹⁄₂ tsp dry mustard powder

¹⁄₂–1 tsp caster sugar, or to taste

salt and freshly ground black pepper

3 tbsp white wine vinegar

120 ml/4 fl oz extra virgin olive oil

Place all the ingredients in a screw top jar and shake vigorously. Use as required.

Other flavours can be made by substituting the vinegar: try raspberry, cider or balsamic vinegar with a little clear honey in place of the sugar. Replace the dry mustard powder with 1 teaspoon of wholegrain mustard. Freshly chopped herbs can also be added to the dressing.

Mayonnaise

Makes 150 ml/¹⁄₄ pint

1 medium egg yolk

¹⁄₄ tsp dry mustard powder

salt and freshly ground black pepper

¹⁄₂ tsp caster sugar

150 ml/¹⁄₄ pt extra virgin olive oil

1 tbsp white wine vinegar or lemon juice

Chocolate Sauce
Makes 150 ml/¹/₄ pint

100 g/4 oz plain dark chocolate

1 tbsp butter

1 tsp golden syrup

75 ml/3 fl oz semi-skimmed milk

Break the chocolate into small pieces and place in a small, heavy based saucepan. Add the remaining ingredients and place over a gentle heat, stirring occasionally until smooth. Pour into a small jug and use as required.

Butterscotch Sauce
Makes 300 ml/¹/₂ pint

75 g/3 oz light muscovado sugar

1 tbsp golden syrup

50 g/2 oz butter

200 ml/7 fl oz single cream

Place the sugar, syrup and butter in a heavy based saucepan and heat gently, stirring occasionally until blended. Stir in the cream and continue to heat, stirring until the sauce is smooth. Use as required.

Syrup Sauce
Makes 150 ml/¹/₄ pint

5 tbsp golden syrup

2 tbsp lemon juice

1 tbsp arrowroot

Pour the syrup and lemon juice into a small pan and add 3 tablespoons of water. Bring to the boil. Blend the arrowroot with 1 tablespoon of water, then stir into the boiling syrup. Cook, stirring, until the sauce thickens and clears. Serve.

Lemon Sauce
Makes 150 ml/¹/₄ pint

Grated rind of 1 large lemon, preferably unwaxed

75 ml/3 fl oz fresh lemon juice, strained

2 tbsp caster sugar

1 tbsp arrowroot

2 tsp butter

Place the grated lemon rind with the juice in a saucepan with 4 tablespoons of water. Stir in the sugar and heat, stirring until the sugar has dissolved. Bring to the boil. Blend the arrowroot with 1 tablespoon of water then blend into the

boiling sauce. Cook, stirring until the sauce thickens and clears. Add the butter and cook for a further 1 minute. Oranges can be used in place of the lemon, or a combination of the two.

Melba Sauce

Makes 300 ml/¹/₂ pint

350 g/12 oz fresh or thawed frozen raspberries
40 g/1¹/₂ oz sugar or to taste
1 tbsp lemon or orange juice

Clean the raspberries if using fresh, then place all the ingredients and 4 tablespoons of water in a heavy based saucepan and place over a gentle heat. Bring to the boil, then reduce the heat and simmer for 5–8 minutes or until the fruits are really soft. Remove from the heat, cool slightly, then blend in a food processor to form a purée. Rub through a fine sieve to remove the pips and use as required.

Jam Sauce

Makes 150 ml/¹/₄ pt

4 tbsp jam, such as raspberry, apricot, strawberry or marmalade
150 ml/¹/₄ pt fruit juice or water
1 tbsp arrowroot
1 tbsp lemon juice

Place the jam and the fruit juice or water in a small pan and heat, stirring until blended. Rub through a fine sieve to remove any pips, return to the pan and bring to the boil. Blend the arrowroot with the lemon juice and stir into the sauce. Cook, stirring until the sauce thickens and clears. If a thicker sauce is required, use half the amount of fruit juice or water.

Custard

Makes 300 ml/¹/₂ pint

300 ml/¹/₂ pt milk
2 tbsp plain white flour
1 medium egg
few drops vanilla extract
1 tbsp butter
1–2 tbsp caster sugar or to taste

Heat the milk to blood heat. Sift the flour into a bowl, make a well in the centre and add the egg. Beat the egg into the flour, drawing the flour in from the sides of the bowl and slowly adding half the warmed milk. When all the flour has been incorporated, beat well to remove any lumps then stir in the remaining milk. Strain into a clean saucepan and place over a gentle heat and cook, stirring until the sauce thickens and coats the back of the wooden spoon. Stir in the vanilla extract, butter and sugar to taste. Stir until blended and use as required.

Stocks

Chicken Stock

Makes 900 ml/1½ pints

1 cooked chicken carcass

1 medium onion, peeled and cut into wedges

1 large carrot, peeled and chopped

1 celery stick, trimmed and chopped

1 bouquet garni

10 peppercorns

4 whole cloves

salt to taste

Remove any large pieces of meat from the carcass and use as required. Break the carcass into small pieces and place in a large saucepan. Add the vegetables, bouquet garni and spices with 1.2 litres/ 2 pints of water and bring to the boil. Cover with a lid, reduce the heat and simmer for 2 hours. If the liquid is evaporating too quickly, reduce the heat under the pan. Cool, strain and allow to cool fully before storing covered in the refrigerator. Store for up to 3 days. Bring to the boil and simmer for 5 minutes before re-using. Freeze if desired in small, freezer-safe tubs.

Beef Stock

Makes 900 ml/1½ pints

450 g/1 lb beef bones, chopped into small chunks

250 g/12 oz shin of beef, fat discarded and cut into small chunks

1 onion, peeled and cut into wedges

1 large carrot, peeled and cut into chunks

1 celery stick, trimmed and chopped

1 bouquet garni

12 black peppercorns

salt to taste

Place the bones and beef in a roasting tin and cook in an oven preheated to 200°C/400°F/Gas Mark 6 for 20 minutes or until sealed and browned. Remove and place in a large saucepan with the remaining ingredients and 1.2 litres/2 pints of water. Bring to the boil, cover with a lid, reduce the heat and simmer very gently for 4 hours. Strain and add salt to taste. Cool, then skim off any fat that rises to the surface. Store in the refrigerator for up to 3 days, boiling for 5 minutes before using. Alternatively, freeze in small, freezer-safe tubs, covered and labelled.

Thoroughly wash the fish bones or cod's head and place in a large saucepan with the vegetables and bouquet garni. Add 900 ml/1½ pints of water and bring to the boil.

Cover with a lid, reduce the heat and simmer for 30 minutes. Strain and add seasoning to taste, then cool and store in the refrigerator. Use within 2 days, bringing to the boil and simmering steadily for 5 minutes before using. If desired, freeze in small, freezer-safe tubs, covered and labelled.

Bouquet Garni

1 celery stick
2 bay leaves
2 sprigs of parsley
1 sprig of thyme
1 sprig of sage

Vegetable Stock

Makes 900 ml/1½ pints

1 tbsp sunflower oil
1 medium onion, peeled and cut into wedges
1 large carrot, peeled and chopped
2 celery sticks, trimmed and chopped
1 small turnip, peeled and chopped, optional
2 bay leaves
10 black peppercorns
3 whole cloves
salt to taste

Cut the celery stick in half and rinse the herbs. Place the herbs on top of one piece of celery and place the second piece of celery on top. Tie securely and use as required.

Heat the oil in a large saucepan and sauté the vegetables for 8 minutes, stirring frequently. Add the bay leaves with the spices and 1.2 litres/2 pints of water and bring to the boil. Cover with a lid, reduce the heat and simmer for 40 minutes. Strain the stock and add salt to taste. Cool, cover and store in the refrigerator for up to 3 days. Alternatively, pour into small, freezer-safe tubs, cover, label and freeze for up to 1 month.

Fish Stock

Makes 600 ml/1 pint

Fish bones or 1 cod's head
1 onion, peeled and cut into wedges
1 celery stick, trimmed and chopped
1 bouquet garni
salt and freshly ground black pepper

Fish

Poached Fish

Clean the fish, remove scales if necessary and rinse thoroughly. Place in a large frying pan with 1 small peeled and sliced onion and carrot, 1 bay leaf, 5 peppercorns and a few parsley stalks. Pour over sufficient cold water to barely cover, then bring to the boil over a medium heat. Reduce the heat to a simmer, cover and cook gently for 8–10 minutes for fillets and 10–15 minutes for whole fish.

This method is suitable for fillets and small whole fish. When the fish is cooked, the flesh should yield easily when pierced with a round bladed knife, and the fish should look opaque.

Grilled Fish

Line a grill rack with tin foil and preheat the grill to medium high just before grilling. Lightly rinse the fish, pat it dry and place on the foil-lined grill rack. Season with salt and pepper and brush lightly with a little oil. Cook under the grill for 8–10 minutes or until cooked, turning the heat down if the fish is cooking too

quickly. Sprinkle with herbs or pour over a little melted butter or herb-flavoured olive oil to serve.

This method is suitable for fresh fish fillets (not smoked), sardines and other small whole fish. Make 3 slashes across whole fish before grilling.

Griddled Fish

Rinse the fish fillet, pat dry and, if desired, marinate in a marinade of your choice for 30 minutes. Heat a griddle pan until smoking and add the fish, skin side down. Cook for 5 minutes, pressing the fish down with a fish slice. Turn the fish over and continue to cook for a further 4–5 minutes or until cooked to personal preference.

Grilling

Grilled Chicken

Line a grill rack with tin foil and preheat the grill to medium high just before cooking. Lightly rinse the chicken piece and pat dry. If wanted, marinate for 30 minutes before cooking. Drain the chicken from the marinade, if using, and place on the foil-lined grill rack. Cook under the preheated grill for 4 minutes on each side. Reduce the heat to medium and continue to cook for a further 10–12 minutes or until thoroughly cooked and the juices run clear. Serve. This method is suitable for boneless, skinless chicken breast portions, which may cook in a slightly shorter time, and also for chicken secured on skewers, thighs, drumsticks, wings and quarters. Small cuts of chicken and spatchcocked poussin will also work well with this method. It is vital that all poultry is thoroughly cooked. All juices should run clear and the flesh should not show any pink. If in doubt, remove from the heat and cut through into the centre with a small sharp knife – if still slightly pink, return to the heat and cook a little longer.

Grilled Sausages

Line a grill rack with tin foil and preheat the grill to high just before cooking. Prick the sausages all over with the tines of a fork and place on the foil-lined grill rack. Place under the preheated grill and cook for 12–18 minutes, turning frequently, until golden brown all over. Turn the heat down halfway through the cooking time. Chipolata sausages will cook in about 12 minutes, whilst large sausages cook under the grill in about 18 minutes.

Cheese on Toast

Preheat the grill to high. Spread freshly-made and buttered toast with a little pickle or ready-made mustard. Finely grate 25 g/1 oz of cheese and pile on top of the toast. Place under the grill and cook for 2–3 minutes or until golden and bubbling. Cut into fingers to serve.

If liked, thinly sliced tomatoes or very thinly sliced onion could be placed under the cheese before grilling. Alternatively, mix the grated cheese with finely chopped spring onions.

Welsh Rarebit

225 g/8 oz mature Cheddar cheese, grated
25 g/1 oz butter
1 tsp dry mustard powder
salt and freshly ground black pepper
few drops Worcestershire sauce
4 tbsp brown ale
freshly-made buttered toast to serve
parsley sprigs to garnish

Preheat the grill to high just before serving. Place all the ingredients in a heavy based saucepan and heat gently, stirring occasionally until melted and creamy. Spoon the mixture onto toast and cook under the preheated grill for 3 minutes or until golden and bubbling. Garnish with parsley and serve immediately.

Salsa (to accompany the Welsh Rarebit)

1 red chilli, deseeded and finely chopped
4 spring onions, trimmed and finely chopped
3 ripe tomatoes, peeled, seeded and finely chopped
1 small ripe avocado, pitted, peeled and finely chopped
1 tbsp finely grated lemon rind
salt and freshly ground black pepper
2 tsp clear honey, warmed
1 tbsp freshly chopped coriander

Mix all the ingredients together, cover and leave for the flavours to infuse for at least 30 minutes. Use as required. Other ingredients can be used to make salsas – try finely diced fruits such as mango, papaya and apple, chopped red onion, chopped skinned peppers, celery, crushed garlic or some chopped dried fruits, such as ready-to-eat apricots, dried cranberries or raisins.

Baking

Pouring Batter/Yorkshire Puddings

100 g/4 oz plain white flour
pinch of salt
2 medium eggs
300 ml/¹/₂ pt whole milk and water mixed

Sift the flour and salt into a mixing bowl and make a well in the centre. Drop the eggs into the well with a little milk. Beat the eggs into the flour, gradually drawing the flour in from the sides of the bowl. Once half the milk has been added, beat well until smooth and free from lumps. Stir in the remaining milk and leave to stand for 30 minutes. Stir before using. Heat 1 tablespoon of oil in a roasting tin or individual Yorkshire Pudding tins in an oven preheated to 220°C/425°F/Gas Mark 7. When the oil is almost smoking, stir the batter then pour into the hot oil. Cook for 30–40 minutes for a large pudding and 18–20 minutes for individual puddings. This batter can also be used for pancakes and, if liked, 25 g/1 oz caster sugar can be added.

Coating Batter/Fritters

100 g/4 oz plain white flour
pinch of salt
1 tbsp sunflower oil
150 ml/¹/₄ pint water
2 medium egg whites

Sift the flour and salt into a mixing bowl and make a well in the centre. Add the oil and half the water and beat until smooth and free from lumps. Gradually beat in the remaining water. Just before using, whisk the egg whites until stiff then stir into the batter and use immediately.

Meringues

Meringue is made from egg whites and sugar, normally caster sugar. As a general rule, allow 1 medium egg white to 50 g/2 oz caster sugar. If liked, a pinch of salt can be added at the beginning of whisking.

Place the egg whites in a clean mixing bowl (any grease in the bowl will prevent the egg white from whisking). Use a balloon or wire whisk, if whisking by hand, or an electric mixer fitted with the balloon wire whisk if not. Whisk the egg whites until stiff. To test if they are stiff enough, turn the bowl upside down – if the egg white does not move, it is ready. Slowly add half the sugar, 1 teaspoon at a time and whisking well after each addition. Once half the sugar has been added, add the remaining sugar and gently stir it in with a metal spoon. Take care not to over-mix.

Whipped Cream (to accompany the Meringues)

Whipping cream, double cream or a combination of single cream and double cream will all whip. If using single and double cream, use one-third single and two-thirds double cream.

Place the cream in a mixing bowl and use a balloon whisk, wire whisk or electric mixer fitter with the balloon whisk attachment. Place the bowl on a damp cloth if whipping by hand. Whip until thickened and soft peaks are formed – this is when the whisk is dragged gently through the cream and lifted out leaving soft peaks in the cream. Whipped cream is ideal for using in soufflés, mousses and other cream desserts. For piping and to use as a filling, whip for a little longer and until cream is slightly stiffer. Take care if using only double cream that you do not over-whip as it will curdle.

Pastry

Shortcrust Pastry
Makes 225 g/8 oz

225 g/8 oz plain white flour

pinch of salt

50 g/2 oz white vegetable fat or lard

50 g/2 oz butter or block margarine

Sift the flour and salt into a mixing bowl. Cut the fats into small pieces and add to the bowl. Rub the fats into the flour using your fingertips until the mixture resembles fine breadcrumbs. Add 1–2 tablespoons of cold water and mix to form a soft, pliable dough. Knead gently on a lightly floured surface until smooth and free from cracks, then wrap and chill for 30 minutes before rolling out on a lightly floured surface. Use as required. Cook in a preheated hot oven (200°C/400°F/Gas Mark 6).

Sweet Shortcrust Pastry (Pâte Sucrée)
Makes 225 g/8 oz

225 g/8 oz plain white flour

150 g/5 oz unsalted butter, softened

2 tbsp caster sugar

1 medium egg yolk

Sift the flour into a mixing bowl, cut the fat into small pieces, add to the bowl and rub into the flour. Stir in the sugar, then mix to form a pliable dough with the egg yolk and about 1 tablespoon of cold water. Wrap, chill and use as required.

Cheese Pastry
Follow the recipe for sweet shortcrust pastry, but omit the sugar and add 1 teaspoon of dried mustard powder and 50 g/2 oz of grated Cheddar cheese.

Rough Puff Pastry
Makes 225 g/8 oz

225 g/8 oz plain white flour

pinch of salt

150 g/5 oz butter, block margarine or lard

squeeze of lemon juice

Sift the flour and salt together in a mixing bowl. Cut the fat into small pieces and add to the bowl. Add the lemon juice and sufficient cold water, about 6–7 tablespoons, and mix with a fork until you have a fairly stiff mixture. Turn out on to a lightly floured surface and roll into an oblong. Fold the bottom

third up to the centre and bring the top third down to the centre. Gently press the edges together. Give the pastry a half turn then roll the pastry out again into an oblong. Repeat the folding, turning and rolling at least four more times, then wrap and leave to rest in a cool place for at least 30 minutes. Use as required. To cook, place in a preheated oven at 220°C/425°F/Gas Mark 7.

Choux Pastry

Makes 225 g/8 oz

75 g/3 oz plain white flour
pinch salt
50 g/2 oz butter
2 medium eggs, beaten

Place the butter and 150 ml/¼ pt water in a heavy based saucepan. Heat gently, stirring until the butter has melted, and bring to the boil. Draw off the heat and add the flour all at once. Beat with a wooden spoon until the mixture forms a ball in the centre. Cool for five minutes. Gradually add the eggs, beating well after each addition until a stiff mixture is formed. Either place in a piping bag fitted with a large nozzle, or shape using two spoons. Cook in a preheated oven at 200°C/400°F/Gas Mark 6 for 15–25 minutes,

depending on size. Remove and make a small slit in the side (see below), then return to the oven and cook for a further five minutes. Remove and leave until cold before filling.

Hot Water Crust Pastry

Makes 450 g/1 lb

450 g/1 lb plain
  white flour
1 tsp salt
100 g/4 oz lard or
  white vegetable fat
150 ml/¼ pt milk and
  water, mixed

Sift the flour and salt together and reserve. Heat the lard or vegetable fat until melted and bring to the boil. Pour into the flour and using a wooden spoon, mix together and beat until the mixture comes together and forms a ball. When cool enough to handle, knead lightly until smooth and pliable.

Use as required, covering the dough with a clean cloth before use. Bake in a preheated oven at 220°C/425°F/Gas Mark 7, or as directed.

Chocolate & Icing

Chocolate

When cooking with chocolate, always use the best chocolate available. The higher the cocoa butter content, the better the flavour and the performance will be.

Melting Chocolate over Water

Break the chocolate into small pieces and place in a small heatproof bowl. Place over a pan of gently simmering water, taking care that the base of the bowl does not touch the simmering water. Heat gently, stirring occasionally until melted. Once melted, remove from the saucepan, stir until smooth, then cool and use as required.

Add any liquid to the chocolate when using this method before commencing to heat. If adding butter, however, add it after melting but before stirring.

Melting Chocolate in a Microwave (650 or 750 watt)

Break the chocolate into small pieces and place in a microwaveable bowl. Heat on 50 per cent heat for $1\frac{1}{4}$ minutes, remove and stir. Continue to heat for 30 seconds each time and stirring until melted.

Melting Chocolate in a Saucepan

Break the chocolate into small pieces and place in a heavy based saucepan. Add either cream or milk with a little butter or liqueur (optional). Heat gently, stirring frequently until the chocolate has melted. Remove and stir until smooth.

If the chocolate becomes hard and grainy during any of these methods due to over-heating, add 1 teaspoon of vegetable fat for every 75 g/3 oz of chocolate and stir until the chocolate becomes soft and smooth. Do not use butter, margarine or oil. Take care that water does not touch the chocolate when melting either in a bowl over water or in the microwave.

Making Caramel

Place 100 g/4 oz granulated sugar in a medium sized, heavy based saucepan. Add 150 ml/¼ pint water and place over a gentle heat. Stir until the sugar has dissolved, then bring to the boil. Boil steadily without stirring for 6–8 minutes or until the sugar becomes golden in colour. Remove and use as required. Plunge the base of the saucepan into cold water to stop the sugar from caramelising further. Take care as the caramel is extremely hot and may spit slightly.

Poaching Fruit

Place 75 g/3 oz sugar in a heavy based saucepan with 150 ml/¼ pint water. Place over a gentle heat and stir occasionally until the sugar has dissolved. Bring to the boil and boil steadily for 5 minutes or until a syrup is formed. Pour into a frying pan, or if the pan is large enough, keep the syrup in the pan. Prepare the fruit to be poached by rinsing and cutting in half and discarding the stones. Add to the syrup and poach gently for 8–10 minutes or until just cooked. Remove from the heat and gently transfer to a serving dish.

This method is suitable for plums, apricots, damsons, greengages, peaches, nectarines, cherries, raspberries, strawberries, blackberries and currants, cored and sliced cooking apples, peeled and cored pears and rhubarb. Alternatively the fruits can be gently poached without sugar. Simply prepare as required and rinse lightly. Half-fill a frying pan with water or a mixture of orange juice and water and bring to the boil. Reduce the heat to a simmer, then add the fruits and cook for 5–10 minutes or until just tender.

Butter Cream Icing

100 g/4 oz softened, unsalted butter or margarine
1 tsp vanilla extract
225 g/8 oz icing sugar, sifted

Cream the butter or margarine with the vanilla extract until soft and creamy. Add the icing sugar, 1 tablespoon at a time, and beat well. Continue until all the icing sugar is incorporated. Beat in 1–2 tablespoons of slightly cooled boiled water or fruit juice to give a smooth, spreadable consistency.

Chocolate Butter Cream

Melt 50 g/2 oz plain dark chocolate and stir into the prepared butter cream, omitting the hot water. Or if preferred, replace 1 tablespoon of the icing sugar with 1 tablespoon of cocoa powder.

Orange/Lemon Butter Cream

Beat 1 tablespoon of finely grated orange or lemon rind into the butter cream and replace the water with fruit juice.

Coffee Butter Cream

Dissolve 1 tablespoon of coffee granules in a little very hot water. Omit the vanilla extract and stir in the dissolved coffee in place of the hot water.

Mocha Butter Cream

Make the coffee butter cream as above and replace 1 tablespoon of the icing sugar with 1 tablespoon of cocoa powder or use melted chocolate.

Glacé Icing

Sift 225 g/8 oz icing sugar into a mixing bowl, then slowly stir in 2–3 tablespoons of hot water and blend to form a spreadable consistency – the icing should coat the back of a wooden spoon.

Other flavours can be made by simply adding 1 tablespoon of cocoa powder to the icing sugar or 1 tablespoon of coffee granules, dissolved in hot water. Fruit-flavoured icing can be made by using orange or lemon juice. To make a coloured icing, simply add a few drops of food colouring.

Mushroom & Sherry Soup

INGREDIENTS

Serves 4

4 slices day old white bread

zest of ½ lemon

1 tbsp lemon juice

salt and freshly ground black pepper

125 g/4 oz assorted wild mushrooms,
   lightly rinsed

125 g/4 oz baby button
   mushrooms, wiped

2 tsp olive oil

1 garlic clove, peeled and crushed

6 spring onions, trimmed
   and diagonally sliced

600 ml/1 pint chicken stock

4 tbsp dry sherry

1 tbsp freshly snipped chives,
   to garnish

HELPFUL HINT

To achieve very fine shreds, use a zester, obtainable from all cook shops. Or thinly peel the fruit with a vegetable peeler, then shred with a small sharp knife. When grating fruit, use a clean, dry pastry brush to remove the rind from the grater.

1 Preheat the oven to 180°C/350°F/Gas Mark 4. Remove the crusts from the bread and cut the bread into small cubes.

2 In a large bowl toss the cubes of bread with the lemon rind and juice, 2 tablespoons of water and plenty of freshly ground black pepper.

3 Spread the bread cubes on to a lightly oiled, large baking tray and bake for 20 minutes until golden and crisp.

4 If the wild mushrooms are small, leave some whole. Otherwise, thinly slice all the mushrooms and reserve.

5 Heat the oil in a saucepan. Add the garlic and spring onions and cook for 1–2 minutes.

6 Add the mushrooms and cook for 3–4 minutes until they start to soften. Add the chicken stock and stir to mix.

7 Bring to the boil, then reduce the heat to a gentle simmer. Cover and cook for 10 minutes.

8 Stir in the sherry, and season to taste with a little salt and pepper. Pour into warmed bowls, sprinkle over the chives, and serve immediately with the lemon croûtons.

2

4

6

Cream of Spinach Soup

INGREDIENTS

Serves 6–8

1 large onion, peeled and chopped

5 large plump garlic cloves, peeled
  and chopped

2 medium potatoes, peeled
  and chopped

750 ml/1¼ pints cold water

1 tsp salt

450 g/1 lb spinach, washed and large
  stems removed

50 g/2 oz butter

3 tbsp flour

750 ml/1¼ pints milk

½ tsp freshly grated nutmeg

freshly ground black pepper

6–8 tbsp crème fraîche
  or soured cream

warm foccacia bread, to serve

1 Place the onion, garlic and potatoes in a large saucepan and cover with the cold water. Add half the salt and bring to the boil. Cover and simmer for 15–20 minutes, or until the potatoes are tender. Remove from the heat and add the spinach. Cover and set aside for 10 minutes.

2 Slowly melt the butter in another saucepan, add the flour and cook over a low heat for about 2 minutes. Remove the saucepan from the heat and add the milk, a little at a time, stirring continuously. Return to the heat and cook, stirring continuously for 5–8 minutes, or until the sauce is smooth and slightly thickened. Add the freshly grated nutmeg, or to taste.

3 Blend the cooled potato and spinach mixture in a food processor or blender to a smooth purée, then return to the saucepan and gradually stir in the white sauce. Season to taste with salt and pepper and gently reheat, taking care not to allow the soup to boil. Ladle into soup bowls and top with spoonfuls of crème fraîche or soured cream. Serve immediately with warm foccacia bread.

HELPFUL HINT

When choosing spinach, always look for fresh, crisp, dark green leaves. Use within 1–2 days of buying and store in a cool place until needed.

Rich Tomato Soup with Roasted Red Peppers

INGREDIENTS

Serves 4

2 tsp light olive oil

700 g/1½ lb red peppers, halved and deseeded

450 g/1 lb ripe plum tomatoes, halved

2 onions, unpeeled and quartered

4 garlic cloves, unpeeled

600 ml/1 pint chicken stock

salt and freshly ground black pepper

4 tbsp soured cream

1 tbsp freshly shredded basil

1 Preheat oven to 200°C/400°F/Gas Mark 6. Lightly oil a roasting tin with 1 teaspoon of the olive oil. Place the peppers and tomatoes cut side down in the roasting tin with the onion quarters and the garlic cloves. Spoon over the remaining oil.

2 Bake in the preheated oven for 30 minutes, or until the skins on the peppers have started to blacken and blister. Allow the vegetables to cool for about 10 minutes, then remove the skins, stalks and seeds from the peppers. Peel away the skins from the tomatoes and onions and squeeze out the garlic.

3 Place the cooked vegetables into a blender or food processor and blend until smooth. Add the stock and blend again to form a smooth purée. Pour the puréed soup through a sieve, if a smooth soup is preferred, then pour into a saucepan. Bring to the boil, simmer gently for 2–3 minutes, and season to taste with salt and pepper. Serve hot with a swirl of soured cream and a sprinkling of shredded basil on the top.

HELPFUL HINT

To help remove the skins of the peppers more easily, remove them from the oven and put immediately into a plastic bag or a bowl covered with clingfilm. Leave until cool enough to handle then skin carefully.

1

2

3

Curried Parsnip Soup

INGREDIENTS

Serves 4

1 tsp cumin seeds
2 tsp coriander seeds
1 tsp oil
1 onion, peeled and chopped
1 garlic clove, peeled and crushed
½ tsp turmeric
¼ tsp chilli powder
1 cinnamon stick
450 g/1 lb parsnips, peeled
  and chopped
1 litre/1¾ pint vegetable stock
salt and freshly ground black pepper
2–3 tbsp low-fat natural yogurt,
  to serve
fresh coriander leaves, to garnish

FOOD FACT

Parsnips vary in colour from pale yellow to a creamy white. They are at their best when they are the size of a large carrot. If larger, remove the central core which can be woody.

1 In a small frying pan, dry-fry the cumin and coriander seeds over a moderately high heat for 1–2 minutes. Shake the pan during cooking until the seeds are lightly toasted.

2 Reserve until cooled. Grind the toasted seeds in a pestle and mortar.

3 Heat the oil in a saucepan. Cook the onion until softened and starting to turn golden.

4 Add the garlic, turmeric, chilli powder and cinnamon stick to the pan. Continue to cook for a further minute.

5 Add the parsnips and stir well. Pour in the stock and bring to the boil. Cover and simmer for 15 minutes or until the parsnips are cooked.

6 Allow the soup to cool. Once cooled, remove the cinnamon stick and discard.

7 Blend the soup in a food processor until very smooth.

8 Transfer to a saucepan and reheat gently. Season to taste with salt and pepper. Garnish with fresh coriander and serve immediately with the yogurt.

1

5

6

Thai Fish Cakes

INGREDIENTS

Serves 4

1 red chilli, deseeded and
  roughly chopped
4 tbsp roughly chopped
  fresh coriander
1 garlic clove, peeled and crushed
2 spring onions, trimmed and
  roughly chopped
1 lemon grass stalk, outer leaves
  discarded and roughly chopped
75 g/3 oz prawns, thawed if frozen
275 g/10 oz cod fillet, skinned, pin
  bones removed and cubed
salt and freshly ground black pepper
sweet chilli dipping sauce, to serve

TASTY TIP

A horseradish accompaniment could be used in place of the sweet chilli sauce if a creamier dip is preferred. Mix together 2 tablespoons of grated horseradish (from a jar) with 3 tablespoons each of Greek yogurt and low-calorie mayonnaise. Add 3 finely chopped spring onions, a squeeze of lime and salt and pepper to taste.

1 Preheat the oven to 190°C/375°F/Gas Mark 5. Place the chilli, coriander, garlic, spring onions and lemon grass in a food processor and blend together.

2 Pat the prawns and cod dry with kitchen paper.

3 Add to the food processor and blend until the mixture is roughly chopped.

4 Season to taste with salt and pepper and blend to mix.

5 Dampen the hands, then shape heaped tablespoons of the mixture into 12 little patties.

6 Place the patties on a lightly oiled baking sheet and cook in the preheated oven for 12–15 minutes or until piping hot and cooked through. Turn the patties over halfway through the cooking time.

7 Serve the fish cakes immediately with the sweet chilli sauce for dipping.

2

2

5

Spicy Beef Pancakes

INGREDIENTS

Serves 4

50 g/2 oz plain flour
pinch of salt
½ tsp Chinese five-spice powder
1 large egg yolk
150 ml/¼ pint milk
4 tsp sunflower oil
slices of spring onion, to garnish

For the spicy beef filling:

1 tbsp sesame oil
4 spring onions, sliced
1 cm/½ inch piece fresh root ginger,
   peeled and grated
1 garlic clove, peeled and crushed
300 g/11 oz sirloin steak, trimmed
   and cut into strips
1 red chilli, deseeded and
   finely chopped
1 tsp sherry vinegar
1 tsp soft dark brown sugar
1 tbsp dark soy sauce

1 Sift the flour, salt and Chinese five-spice powder into a bowl and make a well in the centre. Add the egg yolk and a little of the milk. Gradually beat in, drawing in the flour to make a smooth batter. Whisk in the rest of the milk.

2 Heat 1 teaspoon of the sunflower oil in a small heavy based frying pan. Pour in just enough batter to thinly coat the base of the pan. Cook over a medium heat for 1 minute, or until the underside of the pancake is golden brown.

3 Turn or toss the pancake and cook for 1 minute, or until the other side of the pancake is golden brown. Make 7 more pancakes with the remaining batter. Stack them on a warmed plate as you make them, with greaseproof paper between each pancake. Cover with tinfoil and keep warm in a low oven.

4 Make the filling. Heat a wok or large frying pan, add the sesame oil and when hot, add the spring onions, ginger and garlic and stir-fry for 1 minute. Add the beef strips, stir-fry for 3–4 minutes, then stir in the chilli, vinegar, sugar and soy sauce. Cook for 1 minute, then remove from the heat.

5 Spoon one-eighth of the filling over one half of each pancake. Fold the pancakes in half, then fold in half again. Garnish with a few slices of spring onion and serve immediately.

3

4

5

Courgette & Tarragon Tortilla

INGREDIENTS

Serves 6

700 g/1½ lb potatoes
3 tbsp olive oil
1 onion, peeled and thinly sliced
salt and freshly ground black pepper
1 courgette, trimmed and thinly sliced
6 medium eggs
2 tbsp freshly chopped tarragon
tomato wedges, to serve

FOOD FACT

Almost regarded as the national dish of Spain, this substantial omelette is traditionally made from eggs, potatoes and onions. Here, courgettes and tarragon are added for extra flavour and colour. Use even-sized waxy potatoes, which will not break up during cooking – Maris Bard, Charlotte or Pentland Javelin are all good choices of potato.

1 Peel the potatoes and thinly slice. Dry the slices in a clean tea towel to get them as dry as possible. Heat the oil in a large heavy based pan, add the onion and cook for 3 minutes. Add the potatoes with a little salt and pepper, then stir the potatoes and onion lightly to coat in the oil.

2 Reduce the heat to the lowest possible setting, cover and cook gently for 5 minutes. Turn the potatoes and onion over and continue to cook for a further 5 minutes. Give the pan a shake every now and again to ensure that the potatoes do not stick to the base or burn. Add the courgette, then cover and cook for a further 10 minutes.

3 Beat the eggs and tarragon together and season to taste with salt and pepper. Pour the egg mixture over the vegetables and return to the heat. Cook on a low heat for up to 20–25 minutes, or until there is no liquid egg left on the surface of the tortilla.

4 Turn the tortilla over by inverting the tortilla onto the lid or onto a flat plate. Return the pan to the heat and cook for a final 3–5 minutes, or until the underside is golden brown. If preferred, place the tortilla under a preheated grill for 4 minutes, or until set and golden brown on top. Cut into small squares and serve hot or cold with tomato wedges.

1

3

4

Sweet Potato Crisps with Mango Salsa

INGREDIENTS

Serves 6

For the salsa:

1 large mango, peeled, stoned and
  cut into small cubes
8 cherry tomatoes, quartered
½ cucumber, peeled if preferred and
  finely diced
1 red onion, peeled and
  finely chopped
pinch of sugar
1 red chilli, deseeded and
  finely chopped
2 tbsp rice vinegar
2 tbsp olive oil
grated rind and juice of 1 lime
2 tbsp freshly chopped mint
450 g/1 lb sweet potatoes, peeled
  and thinly sliced
vegetable oil, for deep frying
sea salt

1 To make the salsa, mix the mango with the tomatoes, cucumber and onion. Add the sugar, chilli, vinegar, oil and the lime rind and juice. Mix together thoroughly, cover and leave for 45–50 minutes.

2 Soak the potatoes in cold water for 40 minutes to remove as much of the excess starch as possible. Drain and dry thoroughly in a clean tea towel, or absorbent kitchen paper.

3 Heat the oil to 190°C/375°F in a deep fryer. When at the correct temperature, place half the potatoes in the frying basket, then carefully lower the potatoes into the hot oil and cook for 4–5 minutes, or until they are golden brown, shaking the basket every minute so that they do not stick together.

4 Drain the potato crisps on absorbent kitchen paper, sprinkle with sea salt and place under a preheated moderate grill for a few seconds to dry out. Repeat with the remaining potatoes. Stir the mint into the salsa and serve with the potato crisps.

1

3

4

Ginger & Garlic Potatoes

INGREDIENTS

Serves 4

700 g/1½ lb potatoes

2.5 cm/1 inch piece of root ginger,
  peeled and coarsely chopped

3 garlic cloves, peeled and chopped

½ tsp turmeric

1 tsp salt

½ tsp cayenne pepper

5 tbsp vegetable oil

1 tsp whole fennel seeds

1 large eating apple, cored and diced

6 spring onions, trimmed and
  sliced diagonally

1 tbsp freshly chopped coriander

To serve:

assorted bitter salad leaves

curry flavoured mayonnaise

FOOD FACT

Turmeric is a rhizome that comes from the same family as ginger. When the root is dried, it has a dull yellow appearance and can be ground to a powder. Turmeric powder can be used in a wide range of savoury dishes. It has a warm spicy flavour, and gives food a wonderful golden colour.

1   Scrub the potatoes, then place, unpeeled, in a large saucepan and cover with boiling salted water. Bring to the boil and cook for 15 minutes, then drain and leave the potatoes to cool completely. Peel and cut into 2.5 cm/1 inch cubes.

2   Place the root ginger, garlic, turmeric, salt and cayenne pepper in a food processor and blend for 1 minute. With the motor still running, slowly add 3 tablespoons of water and blend into a paste. Alternatively, pound the ingredients to a paste with a pestle and mortar.

3   Heat the oil in a large heavy based frying pan and when hot, but not smoking, add the fennel seeds and fry for a few minutes. Stir in the ginger paste and cook for 2 minutes, stirring frequently. Take care not to burn the mixture.

4   Reduce the heat, then add the potatoes and cook for 5–7 minutes, stirring frequently, until the potatoes have a golden-brown crust. Add the diced apple and spring onions, then sprinkle with the freshly chopped coriander. Heat through for 2 minutes, then serve on assorted salad leaves with curry flavoured mayonnaise.

Fruits de Mer Stir Fry

INGREDIENTS

Serves 4

450 g/1 lb mixed fresh shellfish, such
  as tiger prawns, squid, scallops
  and mussels
2.5 cm/1 inch piece fresh root ginger
2 garlic cloves, peeled and crushed
2 green chillies, deseeded and
  finely chopped
3 tbsp light soy sauce
2 tbsp olive oil
200 g/7 oz baby sweetcorn, rinsed
200 g/7 oz asparagus tips, trimmed
  and cut in half
200 g/7 oz mangetout, trimmed
2 tbsp plum sauce
4 spring onions, trimmed
  and shredded, to garnish
freshly cooked rice, to serve

1 Prepare the shellfish. Peel the prawns and if necessary remove the thin black veins from the back of the prawns. Lightly rinse the squid rings and clean the scallops if necessary.

2 Remove and discard any mussels that are open. Scrub and debeard the remaining mussels, removing any barnacles from the shells. Cover the mussels with cold water until required.

3 Peel the root ginger and either coarsely grate or shred finely with a sharp knife and place into a small bowl.

4 Add the garlic and chillies to the small bowl, pour in the soy sauce and mix well.

5 Place the mixed shellfish, except the mussels in a bowl and pour over the marinade. Stir, cover and leave for 15 minutes.

6 Heat a wok until hot, then add the oil and heat until almost smoking. Add the prepared vegetables, stir-fry for 3 minutes, then stir in the plum sauce.

7 Add the shellfish and the mussels with the marinade and stir-fry for a further 3–4 minutes, or until the fish is cooked. Discard any mussels that have not opened. Garnish with the spring onions and serve immediately with the freshly cooked rice.

HELPFUL HINT

When stir-frying, it is important that the wok is heated before the oil is added. This ensures that that the food does not stick to the wok.

1

4

7

Sardines with Redcurrants

INGREDIENTS

Serves 4

2 tbsp redcurrant jelly
finely grated rind of 1 lime
2 tbsp medium dry sherry
450 g /1 lb fresh sardines, cleaned
  and heads removed
sea salt and freshly ground
  black pepper
lime wedges, to garnish

To serve:
fresh redcurrants
fresh green salad

TOP TIP

Most fish are sold cleaned but it is easy to do yourself. Using the back of a knife, scrape off the scales from the tail towards the head. Make a small slit along their bellies using a sharp knife. Carefully scrape out the entrails and rinse thoroughly under cold running water. Pat dry with absorbent paper.

1 Preheat the grill and line the grill rack with tinfoil 2–3 minutes before cooking.

2 Warm the redcurrant jelly in a bowl standing over a pan of gently simmering water and stir until smooth. Add the lime rind and sherry to the bowl and stir well until blended.

3 Lightly rinse the sardines and pat dry with absorbent kitchen paper.

4 Place on a chopping board and with a sharp knife make several diagonal cuts across the flesh of each fish. Season the sardines inside the cavities with salt and pepper.

5 Gently brush the warm marinade over the skin and inside the cavities of the sardines.

6 Place on the grill rack and cook under the preheated grill for 8–10 minutes, or until the fish are cooked.

7 Carefully turn the sardines over at least once during grilling. Baste occasionally with the remaining redcurrant and lime marinade. Garnish with the redcurrants. Serve immediately with the salad and lime wedges.

2

4

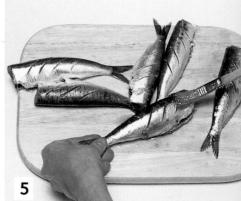

5

Smoked Mackerel & Potato Salad

INGREDIENTS

Serves 4

½ tsp dry mustard powder

1 large egg yolk

salt and freshly ground black pepper

150 ml/¼ pint sunflower oil

1–2 tbsp lemon juice

450 g/1 lb baby new potatoes

25 g/1 oz butter

350 g/12 oz smoked mackerel fillets

4 celery stalks, trimmed and
  finely chopped

3 tbsp creamed horseradish

150 ml/¼ pint crème fraîche

1 Little Gem, rinsed and roughly torn

8 cherry tomatoes, halved

1 Place the mustard powder and egg yolk in a small bowl with salt and pepper and whisk until blended. Add the oil, drop by drop, into the egg mixture, whisking continuously. When the mayonnaise is thick, add the lemon juice, drop by drop, until a smooth, glossy consistency is formed. Reserve.

2 Cook the potatoes in boiling salted water until tender, then drain. Cool slightly, then cut into halves or quarters, depending on size. Return to the saucepan and toss in the butter.

3 Remove the skin from the mackerel fillets and flake into pieces. Add to the potatoes in the saucepan, together with the celery.

4 Blend 4 tablespoons of the mayonnaise with the horseradish and crème fraîche. Season to taste with salt and pepper, then add to the potato and mackerel mixture and stir lightly.

5 Arrange the lettuce and tomatoes on 4 serving plates. Pile the smoked mackerel mixture on top of the lettuce, grind over a little pepper and serve with the remaining mayonnaise.

HELPFUL HINT

When making mayonnaise, ensure that the ingredients are at room temperature, or it may curdle. For speed, it can be made in a food processor: briefly blend the mustard, yolk, seasoning and lemon juice, then with the motor running, slowly pour in the oil.

1

1

3

Battered Cod & Chunky Chips

INGREDIENTS

Serves 4

15 g/½ oz fresh yeast
300 ml/½ pint beer
225 g/8 oz plain flour
1 tsp salt
700 g/1½ lb potatoes
450 ml/¾ pint groundnut oil
4 cod fillets, about 225 g/8 oz each,
  skinned and boned
2 tbsp seasoned plain flour

To garnish:
lemon wedges
sprigs of flat-leaf parsley

To serve:
tomato ketchup
vinegar

HELPFUL HINT

Fresh yeast can be bought in health food shops, large supermarkets with in-store bakeries, and some bakers. Check that it is moist and creamy-coloured and has a strong yeasty smell. If it is dry, discoloured and crumbly, it is probably stale and will not work well.

1 Dissolve the yeast with a little of the beer in a jug and mix to a paste. Pour in the remaining beer, whisking all the time until smooth. Place the flour and salt in a bowl, and gradually pour in the beer mixture, whisking continuously to make a thick smooth batter. Cover the bowl and allow the batter to stand at room temperature for 1 hour.

2 Peel the potatoes and cut into thick slices. Cut each slice lengthways to make chunky chips. Place them in a non-stick frying pan and heat, shaking the pan until all the moisture has evaporated. Turn them onto absorbent kitchen paper to dry off.

3 Heat the oil to 180°C/350°F, then fry the chips a few at a time for 4–5 minutes until crisp and golden. Drain on absorbent kitchen paper and keep warm.

4 Pat the cod fillets dry, then coat in the flour. Dip the floured fillets into the reserved batter. Fry for 2–3 minutes until cooked and crisp, then drain. Garnish with lemon wedges and parsley and serve immediately with the chips, tomato ketchup and vinegar.

Stir-fried Salmon with Peas

INGREDIENTS

Serves 4

450 g/1 lb salmon fillet

salt

6 slices streaky bacon

1 tbsp vegetable oil

50 ml/2 fl oz chicken or fish stock

2 tbsp dark soy sauce

2 tbsp Chinese rice wine or dry sherry

1 tsp sugar

75 g/3 oz frozen peas, thawed

1–2 tbsp freshly shredded mint

1 tsp cornflour

sprigs of fresh mint, to garnish

freshly cooked noodles, to serve

HELPFUL HINT

Sprinkling salmon with salt draws out some of the juices and makes the flesh firmer, so that it remains whole when cooked. Prior to cooking, pat the strips with absorbent kitchen paper to remove as much of the salty liquid as possible. Dark soy sauce is used in this recipe as it is slightly less salty than the light version.

1 Wipe and skin the salmon fillet and remove any pin bones. Slice into 2.5 cm/1 inch strips, place on a plate and sprinkle with salt. Leave for 20 minutes, then pat dry with absorbent kitchen paper and reserve.

2 Remove any cartilage from the bacon, cut into small dice and reserve.

3 Heat a wok or large frying pan over a high heat, then add the oil and when hot, add the bacon and stir-fry for 3 minutes or until crisp and golden. Push to one side and add the strips of salmon. Stir-fry gently for 2 minutes or until the flesh is opaque.

4 Pour the chicken or fish stock, soy sauce and Chinese rice wine or sherry into the wok, then stir in the sugar, peas and freshly shredded mint.

5 Blend the cornflour with 1 tablespoon of water to form a smooth paste and stir into the sauce. Bring to the boil, reduce the heat and simmer for 1 minute, or until slightly thickened and smooth. Garnish and serve immediately with noodles.

Fresh Tuna Salad

INGREDIENTS

Serves 4

225 g/8 oz mixed salad leaves
225 g/8 oz baby cherry tomatoes,
 halved lengthways
125 g/4 oz rocket leaves, washed
2 tbsp groundnut oil
550 g/1¼ lb boned tuna steaks, each
 cut into 4 small pieces
50 g/2 oz piece fresh
 Parmesan cheese

For the dressing:

8 tbsp olive oil
grated zest and juice of
 2 small lemons
1 tbsp wholegrain mustard
salt and freshly ground black pepper

1 Wash the salad leaves and place in a large salad bowl with the cherry tomatoes and rocket and reserve.

2 Heat the wok, then add the oil and heat until almost smoking. Add the tuna, skin-side down, and cook for 4–6 minutes, turning once during cooking, or until cooked and the flesh flakes easily. Remove from the heat and leave to stand in the juices for 2 minutes before removing.

3 Meanwhile make the dressing, place the olive oil, lemon zest and juices and mustard in a small bowl or screw-topped jar and whisk or shake well until blended. Season to taste with salt and pepper.

4 Transfer the tuna to a clean chopping board and flake, then add it to the salad and toss lightly.

5 Using a swivel blade vegetable peeler, peel the piece of Parmesan cheese into shavings. Divide the salad between 4 large serving plates, drizzle the dressing over the salad, then scatter with the Parmesan shavings.

HELPFUL HINT

Bags of mixed salad leaves are available from all major supermarkets. Although they seem expensive, there is very little waste and they do save time. Rinse the leaves before using.

2

3

5

Szechuan Chilli Prawns

INGREDIENTS

Serves 4

450 g/1 lb raw tiger prawns
2 tbsp groundnut oil
1 onion, peeled and sliced
1 red pepper, deseeded and
    cut into strips
1 small red chilli, deseeded and
    thinly sliced
2 garlic cloves, peeled and
    finely chopped
2–3 spring onions, trimmed and
    diagonally sliced
freshly cooked rice or noodles,
    to serve
sprigs of fresh coriander or chilli
    flowers, to garnish

For the chilli sauce:
1 tbsp cornflour
4 tbsp cold fish stock or water
2 tbsp soy sauce
2 tbsp sweet or hot chilli sauce,
    or to taste
2 tsp soft light brown sugar

1 Peel the prawns, leaving the tails attached if you like. Using a sharp knife, remove the black vein along the back of the prawns. Rinse and pat dry with absorbent kitchen paper.

2 Heat a wok or large frying pan, add the oil and when hot, add the onion, pepper and chilli and stir-fry for 4–5 minutes, or until the vegetables are tender but retain a bite. Stir in the garlic and cook for 30 seconds. Using a slotted spoon, transfer to a plate and reserve.

3 Add the prawns to the wok and stir-fry for 1–2 minutes, or until they turn pink and opaque.

4 Blend all the chilli sauce ingredients together in a bowl or jug, then stir into the prawns. Add the reserved vegetables and bring to the boil, stirring constantly. Cook for 1–2 minutes, or until the sauce is thickened and the prawns and vegetables are well coated.

5 Stir in the spring onions, tip on to a warmed platter and garnish with chilli flowers or coriander sprigs. Serve immediately with freshly cooked rice or noodles.

Supreme Baked Potatoes

INGREDIENTS

Serves 4

4 large baking potatoes
40 g/1½ oz butter
1 tbsp sunflower oil
1 carrot, peeled and chopped
2 celery stalks, trimmed and
  finely chopped
200 g can white crab meat
2 spring onions, trimmed and
  finely chopped
salt and freshly ground black pepper
50 g/2 oz Cheddar cheese, grated
tomato salad, to serve

1 Preheat the oven to 200°C/400°F/Gas Mark 6. Scrub the potatoes and prick all over with a fork, or thread 2 potatoes onto 2 long metal skewers. Place the potatoes in the preheated oven for 1–1½ hours, or until soft to the touch. Allow to cool a little, then cut in half.

2 Scoop out the cooked potato and turn into a bowl, leaving a reasonably firm potato shell. Mash the cooked potato flesh, then mix in the butter and mash until the butter has melted.

3 While the potatoes are cooking, heat the oil in a frying pan and cook the carrot and celery for 2 minutes. Cover the pan tightly and continue to cook for another 5 minutes, or until the vegetables are tender.

4 Add the cooked vegetables to the bowl of mashed potato and mix well. Fold in the crab meat and the spring onions, then season to taste with salt and pepper.

5 Pile the mixture back into the potato shells and press in firmly. Sprinkle the grated cheese over the top and return the potato halves to the oven for 12–15 minutes until hot, golden and bubbling. Serve immediately with a tomato salad.

TASTY TIP

Threading the potatoes onto metal skewers helps them to cook more evenly and quickly as heat is transferred via the metal to the centres of the potatoes during cooking. To give the skins a crunchier finish, rub them with a little oil and lightly sprinkle with salt before baking.

2

4

5

Warm Chicken & Potato Salad with Peas & Mint

INGREDIENTS

Serves 4–6

450 g/1 lb new potatoes, peeled
  or scrubbed and cut into
  bite-sized pieces
salt and freshly ground black pepper
2 tbsp cider vinegar
175 g/6 oz frozen garden
  peas, thawed
1 small ripe avocado
4 cooked chicken breasts, about
  450 g/1 lb in weight, skinned
  and diced
2 tbsp freshly chopped mint
2 heads Little Gem lettuce
fresh mint sprigs, to garnish

For the dressing:

2 tbsp raspberry or sherry vinegar
2 tsp Dijon mustard
1 tsp clear honey
50 ml/2 fl oz sunflower oil
50 ml/2 fl oz extra-virgin olive oil

1 Cook the potatoes in lightly salted boiling water for 15 minutes, or until just tender when pierced with the tip of a sharp knife; do not overcook. Rinse under cold running water to cool slightly, then drain and turn into a large bowl. Sprinkle with the cider vinegar and toss gently.

2 Run the peas under hot water to ensure that they are thawed, pat dry with absorbent kitchen paper and add to the potatoes.

3 Cut the avocado in half lengthways and remove the stone. Peel and cut the avocado into cubes and add to the potatoes and peas. Add the chicken and stir together lightly.

4 To make the dressing, place all the ingredients in a screw-top jar, with a little salt and pepper and shake well to mix; add a little more oil if the flavour is too sharp. Pour over the salad and toss gently to coat. Sprinkle in half the mint and stir lightly.

5 Separate the lettuce leaves and spread onto a large shallow serving plate. Spoon the salad on top and sprinkle with the remaining mint. Garnish with mint sprigs and serve.

1

3

4

Turkey & Vegetable Stir Fry

INGREDIENTS

Serves 4

350 g/12 oz mixed vegetables, such
as baby sweetcorn, 1 small red
pepper, pak choi, mushrooms,
broccoli florets and baby carrots
1 red chilli
2 tbsp groundnut oil
350 g/12 oz skinless, boneless turkey
breast, sliced into fine strips across
the grain
2 garlic cloves, peeled and
finely chopped
2.5 cm/1 inch piece fresh root ginger,
peeled and finely grated
3 spring onions, trimmed and
finely sliced
2 tbsp light soy sauce
1 tbsp Chinese rice wine or dry sherry
2 tbsp chicken stock or water
1 tsp cornflour
1 tsp sesame oil
freshly cooked noodles or rice,
to serve

To garnish:

50 g/2 oz toasted cashew nuts
2 spring onions, finely shredded
25 g/1 oz beansprouts

1 Slice or chop the vegetables into small pieces, depending on which
you use. Halve the baby sweetcorn lengthways, deseed and thinly
slice the red pepper, tear or shred the pak choi, slice the mushrooms,
break the broccoli into small florets and cut the carrots into
matchsticks. Deseed and finely chop the chilli.

2 Heat a wok or large frying pan, add the oil and when hot, add
the turkey strips and stir-fry for 1 minute or until they turn white.
Add the garlic, ginger, spring onions and chilli and cook for
a few seconds.

3 Add the prepared carrot, pepper, broccoli and mushrooms and stir-
fry for 1 minute. Add the baby sweetcorn and pak choi and stir-fry
for 1 minute.

4 Blend the soy sauce, Chinese rice wine or sherry and stock or water
and pour over the vegetables. Blend the cornflour with 1 teaspoon
of water and stir into the vegetables, mixing well. Bring to the boil,
reduce the heat, then simmer for 1 minute. Stir in the sesame oil.
Tip into a warmed serving dish, sprinkle with cashew nuts,
shredded spring onions and beansprouts. Serve immediately
with noodles or rice.

Turkey Hash with Potato & Beetroot

INGREDIENTS

Serves 4–6

2 tbsp vegetable oil

50 g/2 oz butter

4 slices streaky bacon, diced or sliced

1 medium onion, peeled and
  finely chopped

450 g/1 lb cooked turkey, diced

450 g/1 lb finely chopped
  cooked potatoes

2–3 tbsp freshly chopped parsley

2 tbsp plain flour

250 g/9 oz cooked medium
  beetroot, diced

green salad, to serve

1 In a large, heavy based frying pan, heat the oil and half the butter over a medium heat until sizzling. Add the bacon and cook for 4 minutes, or until crisp and golden, stirring occasionally. Using a slotted spoon, transfer to a large bowl. Add the onion to the pan and cook for 3–4 minutes, or until soft and golden, stirring frequently.

2 Meanwhile, add the turkey, potatoes, parsley and flour to the cooked bacon in the bowl. Stir and toss gently, then fold in the diced beetroot.

3 Add half the remaining butter to the frying pan and then the turkey vegetable mixture. Stir, then spread the mixture to evenly cover the bottom of the frying pan. Cook for 15 minutes, or until the underside is crisp and brown, pressing the hash firmly into a cake with a spatula. Remove from the heat.

4 Invert a large plate over the frying pan and, holding the plate and frying pan together with an oven glove, turn the hash out onto the plate. Heat the remaining butter in the pan, slide the hash back into the pan and cook for 4 minutes, or until crisp and brown on the other side. Invert onto the plate again and serve immediately with a green salad.

TASTY TIP

A hash is usually made just with potatoes, but here they are combined with ruby red beetroot, which adds vibrant colour and a sweet earthy flavour to the dish. Make sure that you buy plainly cooked beetroot, rather than the type preserved in vinegar.

2

3

3

Beef Fajitas with Avocado Sauce

INGREDIENTS

Serves 3–6

2 tbsp sunflower oil

450 g/1 lb beef fillet or rump steak,
  trimmed and cut into thin strips

2 garlic cloves, peeled and crushed

1 tsp ground cumin

¼ tsp cayenne pepper

1 tbsp paprika

230 g can chopped tomatoes

215 g can red kidney beans, drained

1 tbsp freshly chopped coriander

1 avocado, peeled, pitted
  and chopped

1 shallot, peeled and chopped

1 large tomato, skinned, deseeded
  and chopped

1 red chilli, diced

1 tbsp lemon juice

6 large flour tortilla pancakes

3–4 tbsp soured cream

green salad, to serve

HELPFUL HINT

The avocado sauce should not be made too far in advance, as it has a tendency to discolour. If it is necessary to make it some time ahead, the surface of the sauce should be covered with clingfilm.

1 Heat the wok, add the oil, then stir-fry the beef for 3–4 minutes. Add the garlic and spices and continue to cook for a further 2 minutes. Stir the tomatoes into the wok, bring to the boil, cover and simmer gently for 5 minutes.

2 Meanwhile, blend the kidney beans in a food processor until slightly broken up, then add to the wok. Continue to cook for a further 5 minutes, adding 2–3 tablespoons of water. The mixture should be thick and fairly dry. Stir in the chopped coriander.

3 Mix the chopped avocado, shallot, tomato, chilli and lemon juice together. Spoon into a serving dish and reserve.

4 When ready to serve, warm the tortillas and spread with a little soured cream. Place a spoonful of the beef mixture on top, followed by a spoonful of the avocado sauce, then roll up. Repeat until all the mixture is used up. Serve immediately with a green salad.

Pasta with Beef, Capers & Olives

INGREDIENTS

Serves 4

2 tbsp olive oil

300 g/11 oz rump steak, trimmed and
  cut into strips

4 spring onions, trimmed and sliced

2 garlic cloves, peeled and chopped

2 courgettes, trimmed and
  cut into strips

1 red pepper, deseeded and
  cut into strips

2 tsp freshly chopped oregano

2 tbsp capers, drained and rinsed

4 tbsp pitted black olives, sliced

400 g can chopped tomatoes

salt and freshly ground black pepper

450 g/1 lb fettuccine

1 tbsp freshly chopped parsley,
  to garnish

TASTY TIP

Make sure that the oil in the pan is
hot so that the strips of beef sizzle
when added. Pat the beef dry with
absorbent kitchen paper and cook
it in two batches. Tip the first
batch on to a plate and reserve
while cooking the second, then
return to the pan with any juices.

1 Heat the olive oil in a large frying pan over a high heat. Add the
   steak and cook, stirring, for 3–4 minutes, or until browned. Remove
   from the pan using a slotted spoon and reserve.

2 Lower the heat, add the spring onions and garlic to the pan
   and cook for 1 minute. Add the courgettes and pepper and cook
   for 3–4 minutes.

3 Add the oregano, capers and olives to the pan with the chopped
   tomatoes. Season to taste with salt and pepper, then simmer for
   7 minutes, stirring occasionally. Return the beef to the pan and
   simmer for 3–5 minutes, or until the sauce has thickened slightly.

4 Meanwhile, bring a large pan of lightly salted water to a rolling boil.
   Add the pasta and cook according to the packet instructions, or
   until 'al dente'.

5 Drain the pasta thoroughly. Return to the pan and add the beef
   sauce. Toss gently until the pasta is lightly coated. Tip into a
   warmed serving dish or onto individual plates. Sprinkle with
   chopped parsley and serve immediately.

Chilli Beef

INGREDIENTS

Serves 4

550 g/1¼ lb beef rump steak
2 tbsp groundnut oil
2 carrots, peeled and cut
  into matchsticks
125 g/4 oz mangetout, shredded
125 g/4 oz beansprouts
1 green chilli, deseeded and chopped
2 tbsp sesame seeds
freshly cooked rice, to serve

For the marinade:

1 garlic clove, peeled and chopped
3 tbsp soy sauce
1 tbsp sweet chilli sauce
4 tbsp groundnut oil

FOOD FACT

Chillies have become a favourite Chinese ingredient, especially in Szechuan. Chilli sauce is a mixture of crushed fresh chillies, plums, vinegar and salt. It is available in several varieties: extra hot, hot or sweet, as used here, which is the mildest version. Chilli sauce may be used as a marinade or as a dip.

1 Using a sharp knife, trim the beef, discarding any fat or gristle, then cut into thin strips and place in a shallow dish. Combine all the marinade ingredients in a bowl and pour over the beef. Turn the beef in the marinade until coated evenly, cover with clingfilm and leave to marinate in the refrigerator for at least 30 minutes.

2 Heat a wok or large frying pan, add the groundnut oil and heat until almost smoking, then add the carrots and stir-fry for 3–4 minutes, or until softened. Add the mangetout and stir-fry for a further 1 minute. Using a slotted spoon, transfer the vegetables to a plate and keep warm.

3 Lift the beef strips from the marinade, shaking to remove excess marinade. Reserve the marinade. Add the beef to the wok and stir-fry for 3 minutes or until browned all over.

4 Return the stir-fried vegetables to the wok together with the beansprouts, chilli and sesame seeds and cook for 1 minute. Stir in the reserved marinade and stir-fry for 1–2 minutes or until heated through. Tip into a warmed serving dish or spoon onto individual plates and serve immediately with freshly cooked rice.

1

2

4

Lamb Arrabbiata

INGREDIENTS

Serves 4

4 tbsp olive oil
450 g/1 lb lamb fillets, cubed
1 large onion, peeled and sliced
4 garlic cloves, peeled and
  finely chopped
1 red chilli, deseeded and
  finely chopped
400 g can chopped tomatoes
175 g/6 oz pitted black olives, halved
150 ml/¼ pint white wine
salt and freshly ground black pepper
275 g/10 oz farfalle pasta
1 tsp butter
4 tbsp freshly chopped parsley,
  plus 1 tbsp to garnish

FOOD FACT

When cooking pasta, remember to use a very large saucepan so that the pasta has plenty of time to move around freely. Once the water has come to the boil, add the pasta, stir, cover with a lid and return to the boil. The lid can then be removed so that the water does not boil over.

1 Heat 2 tablespoons of the olive oil in a large frying pan and cook the lamb for 5–7 minutes, or until sealed. Remove from the pan using a slotted spoon and reserve.

2 Heat the remaining oil in the pan, add the onion, garlic and chilli and cook until softened. Add the tomatoes, bring to the boil, then simmer for 10 minutes.

3 Return the browned lamb to the pan with the olives and pour in the wine. Bring the sauce back to the boil, reduce the heat then simmer, uncovered, for 15 minutes, until the lamb is tender. Season to taste with salt and pepper.

4 Meanwhile, bring a large pan of lightly salted water to a rolling boil. Add the pasta and cook according to the packet instructions, or until 'al dente'.

5 Drain the pasta, toss in the butter, then add to the sauce and mix lightly. Stir in 4 tablespoons of the chopped parsley, then tip into a warmed serving dish. Sprinkle with the remaining parsley and serve immediately.

2

3

5

Hot Salami & Vegetable Gratin

INGREDIENTS

Serves 4

350 g/12 oz carrots
175 g/6 oz fine green beans
250 g/9 oz asparagus tips
175 g/6 oz frozen peas
225 g/8 oz Italian salami
1 tbsp olive oil
1 tbsp freshly chopped mint
25 g/1 oz butter
150 g/5 oz baby spinach leaves
150 ml/¼ pint double cream
salt and freshly ground black pepper
1 small or ½ an olive ciabatta loaf
75 g/3 oz Parmesan cheese, grated
green salad, to serve

1 Preheat oven to 200°C/400°F/Gas Mark 6. Peel and slice the carrots, trim the beans and asparagus and reserve. Cook the carrots in a saucepan of lightly salted, boiling water for 5 minutes. Add the remaining vegetables, except the spinach, and cook for about a further 5 minutes, or until tender. Drain and place in an ovenproof dish.

2 Discard any skin from the outside of the salami, if necessary, then chop roughly. Heat the oil in a frying pan and fry the salami for 4–5 minutes, stirring occasionally, until golden. Using a slotted spoon, transfer the salami to the ovenproof dish and scatter over the mint.

3 Add the butter to the frying pan and cook the spinach for 1–2 minutes, or until just wilted. Stir in the double cream and season well with salt and pepper. Spoon the mixture over the vegetables.

4 Whizz the ciabatta loaf in a food processor to make breadcrumbs. Stir in the Parmesan cheese and sprinkle over the vegetables. Bake in the preheated oven for 20 minutes, until golden and heated through. Serve with a green salad.

TASTY TIP

Prepare this dish ahead up to the end of step 3 and refrigerate until ready to cook, then top with breadcrumbs and bake, adding about 5 minutes to the final cooking time.

1

2

4

Leek & Ham Risotto

INGREDIENTS

Serves 4

1 tbsp olive oil

25 g/1 oz butter

1 medium onion, peeled and
finely chopped

4 leeks, trimmed and thinly sliced

1½ tbsp freshly chopped thyme

350 g/12 oz Arborio rice

1.4 litres/2¼ pints vegetable or
chicken stock, heated

225 g/8 oz cooked ham

175 g/6 oz peas, thawed if frozen

50 g/2 oz Parmesan cheese, grated

salt and freshly ground black pepper

HELPFUL HINT

Risotto should take about 15 minutes to cook, so taste it after this time – the rice should be creamy with just a slight bite to it. If it is not quite ready, continue adding the stock, a little at a time, and cook for a few more minutes. Stop as soon as it tastes ready as you do not have to add all of the liquid.

1 Heat the oil and half the butter together in a large saucepan. Add the onion and leeks and cook over a medium heat for 6–8 minutes, stirring occasionally, until soft and beginning to colour. Stir in the thyme and cook briefly.

2 Add the rice and stir well. Continue stirring over a medium heat for about 1 minute until the rice is glossy. Add a ladleful or two of the stock and stir well until the stock is absorbed. Continue adding stock, a ladleful at a time, and stirring well between additions, until about two-thirds of the stock has been added.

3 Meanwhile, either chop or finely shred the ham, then add to the saucepan of rice together with the peas. Continue adding ladlefuls of stock, as described in step 2, until the rice is tender and the ham is heated through thoroughly.

4 Add the remaining butter, sprinkle over the Parmesan cheese and season to taste with salt and pepper. When the butter has melted and the cheese has softened, stir well to incorporate. Taste and adjust the seasoning, then serve immediately.

1

2

3

Pork Sausages with Onion Gravy & Best–ever Mash

INGREDIENTS

Serves 4

50 g/2 oz butter

1 tbsp olive oil

2 large onions, peeled and
  thinly sliced

pinch of sugar

1 tbsp freshly chopped thyme

1 tbsp plain flour

100 ml/3½ fl oz Madeira

200 ml/7 fl oz vegetable stock

8–12 good-quality butchers pork
  sausages, depending on size

For the mash:

900 g/2 lb floury potatoes, peeled

75 g/3 oz butter

4 tbsp crème fraîche or soured cream

salt and freshly ground black pepper

HELPFUL HINT

There is a huge range of regional pork sausages to choose from. Try meaty Cambridge sausages packed with herbs and spices, or Cumberland sausages made form coarsely chopped pork and black pepper.

1 Melt the butter with the oil and add the onions. Cover and cook gently for about 20 minutes until the onions have collapsed. Add the sugar and stir well. Uncover and continue to cook, stirring often, until the onions are very soft and golden. Add the thyme, stir well, then add the flour, stirring. Gradually add the Madeira and the stock. Bring to the boil and simmer gently for 10 minutes.

2 Meanwhile, put the sausages in a large frying pan and cook over a medium heat for about 15–20 minutes, turning often, until golden brown and slightly sticky all over.

3 For the mash, boil the potatoes in plenty of lightly salted water for 15–18 minutes until tender. Drain well and return to the saucepan. Put the saucepan over a low heat to allow the potatoes to dry thoroughly. Remove from the heat and add the butter, crème fraîche and salt and pepper. Mash thoroughly. Serve the potato mash topped with the sausages and onion gravy.

1

2

3

Pasta & Pork Ragù

INGREDIENTS

Serves 4

1 tbsp sunflower oil
1 leek, trimmed and thinly sliced
225 g/8 oz pork fillet, diced
1 garlic clove, peeled and crushed
2 tsp paprika
¼ tsp cayenne pepper
150 ml/¼ pint white wine
600 ml/1 pint vegetable stock
400g can borlotti beans, drained
  and rinsed
2 carrots, peeled and diced
salt and freshly ground black pepper
225 g/8 oz fresh egg tagliatelle
1 tbsp freshly chopped parsley,
  to garnish
crème fraîche, to serve

HELPFUL HINT

Pork fillet, also known as tenderloin, is a very lean and tender cut of pork. It needs little cooking time, so is perfect for this quick and simple dish. Rump or sirloin steak or boneless skinned chicken breast, cut into thin strips, could be used instead, if preferred.

1   Heat the sunflower oil in a large frying pan. Add the sliced leek and cook, stirring frequently, for 5 minutes, or until softened. Add the pork and cook, stirring, for 4 minutes, or until sealed.

2   Add the crushed garlic, paprika and cayenne pepper to the pan and stir until all the pork is lightly coated in the garlic and pepper mixture.

3   Pour in the wine and 450 ml/¾ pint of the vegetable stock. Add the borlotti beans and carrots and season to taste with salt and pepper. Bring the sauce to the boil, then lower the heat and simmer for 5 minutes.

4   Meanwhile, place the egg tagliatelle in a large saucepan of lightly salted, boiling water, cover and simmer for 5 minutes, or until the pasta is cooked 'al dente'.

5   Drain the pasta, then add to the pork ragù and toss well. Adjust the seasoning, then tip into a warmed serving dish. Sprinkle with chopped parsley and serve with a little crème fraîche.

Pork Goulash & Rice

INGREDIENTS

Serves 4

700 g/1½ lb boneless pork rib chops
1 tbsp olive oil
2 onions, peeled and
   roughly chopped
1 red pepper, deseeded and
   sliced thinly
1 garlic clove, peeled and crushed
1 tbsp plain flour
1 rounded tbsp paprika
400 g can chopped tomatoes
salt and freshly ground black pepper
250 g/9 oz long-grain white rice
450 ml/¾ pint chicken stock
sprigs of fresh flat-leaf parsley,
   to garnish
150 ml/¼ pint soured cream,
   to serve

FOOD FACT

Paprika is the ground red powder from the dried pepper Capsicum annum and is a vital ingredient of goulash, giving it a distinctive colour and taste.

1   Preheat the oven to 140°C/275°F/Gas Mark 1. Cut the pork into large cubes, about 4 cm/1½ inches square. Heat the oil in a large flameproof casserole dish and brown the pork in batches over a high heat, transferring the cubes to a plate as they brown.

2   Over a medium heat, add the onions and pepper and cook for about 5 minutes, stirring regularly, until they begin to brown. Add the garlic and return the meat to the casserole dish along with any juices on the plate. Sprinkle in the flour and paprika and stir well to soak up the oil and juices.

3   Add the tomatoes and season to taste with salt and pepper. Bring slowly to the boil, cover with a tight-fitting lid and cook in the preheated oven for 1½ hours.

4   Meanwhile, rinse the rice in several changes of water until the water remains relatively clear. Drain well and put into a saucepan with the chicken stock or water and a little salt. Cover tightly and bring to the boil. Turn the heat down as low as possible and cook for 10 minutes without removing the lid. After 10 minutes, remove from the heat and leave for a further 10 minutes, without removing the lid. Fluff with a fork.

5   When the meat is tender, stir in the soured cream lightly to create a marbled effect, or serve separately. Garnish with parsley and serve immediately with the rice.

Sweetcorn Fritters

INGREDIENTS

Serves 4

4 tbsp groundnut oil

1 small onion, peeled and
   finely chopped

1 red chilli, deseeded and
   finely chopped

1 garlic clove, peeled and crushed

1 tsp ground coriander

325 g can sweetcorn

6 spring onions, trimmed and
   finely sliced

1 medium egg, lightly beaten

salt and freshly ground black pepper

3 tbsp plain flour

1 tsp baking powder

spring onion curls, to garnish

Thai-style chutney, to serve

HELPFUL HINT

To make a spring onion curl, trim off the root and some green top to leave 10 cm/4 inches. Make a 3 cm/1¼ inch cut down from the top, then make another cut at a right angle to the first cut. Continue making fine cuts. Soak the spring onions in iced water for 20 minutes.

1 Heat 1 tablespoon of the groundnut oil in a frying pan, add the onion and cook gently for 7–8 minutes or until beginning to soften. Add the chilli, garlic and ground coriander and cook for 1 minute, stirring continuously. Remove from the heat.

2 Drain the sweetcorn and tip into a mixing bowl. Lightly mash with a potato masher to break down the corn a little. Add the cooked onion mixture to the bowl with the spring onions and beaten egg. Season to taste with salt and pepper, then stir to mix together. Sift the flour and baking powder over the mixture and stir in.

3 Heat 2 tablespoons of the groundnut oil in a large frying pan. Drop 4 or 5 heaped teaspoonfuls of the sweetcorn mixture into the pan, and using a fish slice or spatula, flatten each to make a 1 cm/½ inch thick fritter.

4 Fry the fritters for 3 minutes, or until golden brown on the underside, turn over and fry for a further 3 minutes, or until cooked through and crisp.

5 Remove the fritters from the pan and drain on absorbent kitchen paper. Keep warm while cooking the remaining fritters, adding a little more oil if needed. Garnish with spring onion curls and serve immediately with a Thai-style chutney.

Tagliatelle with Broccoli & Sesame

INGREDIENTS

Serves 2

225 g/8 oz broccoli, cut into florets
125 g/4 oz baby corn
175 g/6 oz dried tagliatelle
1½ tbsp tahini paste
1 tbsp dark soy sauce
1 tbsp dark muscovado sugar
1 tbsp red wine vinegar
1 tbsp sunflower oil
1 garlic clove, peeled and
   finely chopped
2.5 cm/1 inch piece fresh root ginger,
   peeled and shredded
½ tsp dried chilli flakes
salt and freshly ground black pepper
1 tbsp toasted sesame seeds
slices of radish, to garnish

1. Bring a large saucepan of salted water to the boil and add the broccoli and corn. Return the water to the boil then remove the vegetables at once using a slotted spoon, reserving the water. Plunge them into cold water and drain well. Dry on kitchen paper and reserve.

2. Return the water to the boil. Add the tagliatelle and cook until 'al dente' or according to the packet instructions. Drain well. Run under cold water until cold, then drain well again.

3. Place the tahini, soy sauce, sugar and vinegar into a bowl. Mix well, then reserve. Heat the oil in a wok or large frying pan over a high heat and add the garlic, ginger and chilli flakes and stir-fry for about 30 seconds. Add the broccoli and baby corn and continue to stir-fry for about 3 minutes.

4. Add the tagliatelle to the wok along with the tahini mixture and stir together for a further 1–2 minutes until heated through. Season to taste with salt and pepper. Sprinkle with sesame seeds, garnish with the radish slices and serve immediately.

FOOD FACT

Tahini is made from ground sesame seeds and is generally available in large supermarkets and Middle Eastern shops. It is most often used in hummus.

1

3

4

Vegetable Biryani

INGREDIENTS

Serves 4

2 tbsp vegetable oil, plus a little extra
for brushing

2 large onions, peeled and thinly
sliced lengthways

2 garlic cloves, peeled and
finely chopped

2.5 cm/1 inch piece fresh root ginger,
peeled and finely grated

1 small carrot, peeled and cut
into sticks

1 small parsnip, peeled and diced

1 small sweet potato, peeled
and diced

1 tbsp medium curry paste

225 g/8 oz basmati rice

4 ripe tomatoes, peeled, deseeded
and diced

600 ml/1 pint vegetable stock

175 g/6 oz cauliflower florets

50 g/2 oz peas, thawed if frozen

salt and freshly ground black pepper

To garnish:

roasted cashew nuts

raisins

fresh coriander leaves

1 Preheat the oven to 200°C/400°F/Gas Mark 6. Put 1 tablespoon of the vegetable oil in a large bowl with the onions and toss to coat. Lightly brush or spray a non-stick baking sheet with a little more oil. Spread half the onions onto the baking sheet and cook at the top of the preheated oven for 25–30 minutes, stirring regularly, until golden and crisp. Remove from the oven and reserve for the garnish.

2 Meanwhile, heat a large flameproof casserole dish over a medium heat and add the remaining oil and onions. Cook for 5–7 minutes until softened and starting to brown. Add a little water if they start to stick. Add the garlic and ginger and cook for another minute, then add the carrot, parsnip and sweet potato. Cook the vegetables for a further 5 minutes. Add the curry paste and stir for a minute until everything is coated, then stir in the rice and tomatoes. After 2 minutes add the stock and stir well. Bring to the boil, cover and simmer over a very gentle heat for about 10 minutes.

3 Add the cauliflower and peas and cook for 8–10 minutes, or until the rice is tender. Season to taste with salt and pepper. Serve garnished with the crispy onions, cashew nuts, raisins and coriander.

Baked Aubergines with Tomato & Mozzarella

INGREDIENTS

Serves 4

3 medium aubergines, trimmed and sliced
salt and freshly ground black pepper
4–6 tbsp olive oil
450 g/1 lb fresh turkey mince
1 onion, peeled and chopped
2 garlic cloves, peeled and chopped
2 x 400 g cans cherry tomatoes
1 tbsp fresh mixed herbs
200 ml/7 fl oz red wine
350 g/12 oz macaroni
5 tbsp freshly chopped basil
125 g/4 oz mozzarella cheese, drained and chopped
50 g/2 oz freshly grated Parmesan cheese

HELPFUL HINT

Aubergines are salted to remove bitterness, although they are now less bitter. Salting also removes moisture so they absorb less oil when fried.

1 Preheat the oven to 200°C/400°F/Gas Mark 6, 15 minutes before cooking. Place the aubergine slices in a colander and sprinkle with salt. Leave for 1 hour or until the juices run clear. Rinse and dry on absorbent kitchen paper.

2 Heat 3–5 tablespoons of the olive oil in a large frying pan and cook the prepared aubergines in batches for 2 minutes on each side, or until softened. Remove and drain on absorbent kitchen paper.

3 Heat 1 tablespoon of olive oil in a saucepan, add the turkey mince and cook for 5 minutes, or until browned and sealed.

4 Add the onion to the pan and cook for 5 minutes, or until softened. Add the chopped garlic, the tomatoes and mixed herbs. Pour in the wine and season to taste with salt and pepper. Bring to the boil, lower the heat then simmer for 15 minutes, or until thickened.

5 Meanwhile, bring a large pan of lightly salted water to a rolling boil. Add the macaroni and cook according to the packet instructions, or until 'al dente'. Drain thoroughly.

6 Spoon half the tomato mixture into a lightly oiled ovenproof dish. Top with half the aubergine, pasta and chopped basil, then season lightly. Repeat the layers, finishing with a layer of aubergine. Sprinkle with the mozzarella and Parmesan cheeses, then bake in the preheated oven for 30 minutes, or until golden and bubbling. Serve immediately.

Four-cheese Tagliatelle

INGREDIENTS

Serves 4

300 ml/½ pint whipping cream
4 garlic cloves, peeled and
  lightly bruised
75 g/3 oz fontina cheese, diced
75 g/3 oz Gruyère cheese, grated
75 g/3 oz mozzarella cheese,
  preferably, diced
50 g/2 oz Parmesan cheese, grated,
  plus extra to serve
salt and freshly ground black pepper
275 g/10 oz fresh green tagliatelle
1–2 tbsp freshly snipped chives
fresh basil leaves, to garnish

1 Place the whipping cream with the garlic cloves in a medium pan and heat gently until small bubbles begin to form around the edge of the pan. Using a slotted spoon, remove and discard the garlic cloves.

2 Add all the cheeses to the pan and stir until melted. Season with a little salt and a lot of black pepper. Keep the sauce warm over a low heat, but do not allow to boil.

3 Meanwhile, bring a large pan of lightly salted water to the boil. Add the taglietelle, return to the boil and cook for 2–3 minutes, or until 'al dente'.

4 Drain the pasta thoroughly and return to the pan. Pour the sauce over the pasta, add the chives then toss lightly until well coated. Tip into a warmed serving dish or spoon onto individual plates. Garnish with a few basil leaves and serve immediately with extra Parmesan cheese.

FOOD FACT

Tagliatelle comes from Bologna, where it is usually served with a meat sauce. Green tagliatelle is generally flavoured with spinach, but it is also available flavoured with fresh herbs, which would go particularly well with the rich cheese sauce in this recipe.

Fruit Salad

INGREDIENTS

Serves 4

125 g/4 oz caster sugar

3 oranges

700 g/1½ lb lychees, peeled and stoned

1 small mango

1 small pineapple

1 papaya

4 pieces stem ginger in syrup

4 tbsp stem ginger syrup

125 g/4 oz Cape gooseberries

125 g/4 oz strawberries, hulled

½ tsp almond essence

To decorate:

lime zest

mint leaves

1 Place the sugar and 300 ml/½ pint of water in a small pan and heat, gently stirring until the sugar has dissolved. Bring to the boil and simmer for 2 minutes. Once a syrup has formed, remove from the heat and allow to cool.

2 Using a sharp knife, cut away the skin from the oranges, then slice thickly. Cut each slice in half and place in a serving dish with the syrup and lychees.

3 Peel the mango, then cut into thick slices around each side of the stone. Discard the stone and cut the slices into bite-sized pieces and add to the syrup.

4 Using a sharp knife again, carefully cut away the skin from the pineapple.

5 Remove the central core using the knife or an apple corer, then cut the pineapple into segments and add to the syrup.

6 Peel the papaya, then cut in half and remove the seeds. Cut the flesh into chunks, slice the ginger into matchsticks and add with the ginger syrup to the fruit in the syrup.

7 Prepare the Cape gooseberries by removing the thin, papery skins and rinsing lightly. Add to the syrup.

8 Halve the strawberries, add to the fruit with the almond essence and chill for 30 minutes. Scatter with mint leaves and lime zest to decorate and serve.

FOOD FACT

A fruit salad is the perfect end to a good meal because it refreshes the palate and is also packed full of vitamins.

2

3

5

Fruity Roulade

INGREDIENTS

Serves 4

For the sponge:

3 medium eggs

75 g/3 oz caster sugar

75 g/3 oz plain flour, sieved

1–2 tbsp caster sugar for sprinkling

For the filling:

125 g/4 oz Quark

125 g/4 oz half-fat Greek yogurt

25 g/1 oz caster sugar

1 tbsp orange liqueur (optional)

grated rind of 1 orange

125 g/4 oz strawberries, hulled and
   cut into quarters

To decorate:

strawberries

sifted icing sugar

FOOD FACT

Quark is a soft unripened cheese with the flavour and texture of soured cream. It comes in 2 varieties, low-fat and non-fat. Quark can be used as a sour cream substitute to top baked potatoes, or in dips and cheesecakes.

1 Preheat the oven to 220°C/425°F/Gas Mark 7. Lightly oil and line a 33 x 23 cm/13 x 9 inch Swiss roll tin with greaseproof or baking parchment paper.

2 Using an electric whisk, whisk the eggs and sugar until the mixture is double in volume and leaves a trail across the top.

3 Fold in the flour with a metal spoon or rubber spatula. Pour into the prepared tin and bake in the preheated oven for 10–12 minutes, until well risen and golden.

4 Place a whole sheet of greaseproof or baking parchment paper out on a flat work surface and sprinkle evenly with caster sugar.

5 Turn the cooked sponge out on to the paper, discard the paper, trim the sponge and roll up encasing the paper inside. Reserve until cool.

6 To make the filling, mix together the Quark, yogurt, caster sugar, liqueur (if using) and orange rind. Unroll the roulade and spread over the mixture. Scatter over the strawberries and roll up.

7 Decorate the roulade with the strawberries. Dust with the icing sugar and serve.

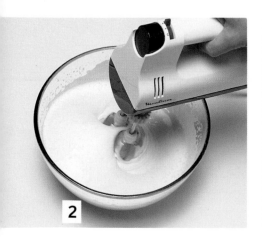

2

5

6

Frozen Mississippi Mud Pie

INGREDIENTS

Cuts into 6–8 slices

1 quantity **Ginger Crumb Crust**
600 ml/1 pint **chocolate ice cream**
600 ml/1 pint **coffee-flavoured**
 ice cream

For the chocolate topping:

175 g/6 oz **plain dark**
 chocolate, chopped
50 ml/2 fl oz **single cream**
1 tbsp **golden syrup**
1 tsp **vanilla essence**
50 g/2 oz **coarsely grated white and**
 milk chocolate

HELPFUL HINT

Use the best-quality ice cream that is available for this recipe. Look for chocolate ice cream with added ingredients such as chocolate chips, pieces of toffee or rippled chocolate. If preferred you can add some raspberries, chopped nuts or small pieces of chopped white chocolate to both the chocolate and coffee ice cream.

1 Prepare the crumb crust and use to line a 23 cm/9 inch loose-based flan tin and freeze for 30 minutes.

2 Soften the ice creams at room temperature for about 25 minutes. Spoon the chocolate ice cream into the crumb crust, spreading it evenly over the base, then spoon the coffee ice cream over the chocolate ice cream, mounding it slightly in the centre. Return to the freezer to refreeze the ice cream.

3 For the topping, heat the dark chocolate with the cream, golden syrup and vanilla essence in a saucepan. Stir until the chocolate has melted and is smooth. Pour into a bowl and chill in the refrigerator, stirring occasionally, until cold but not set.

4 Spread the cooled chocolate mixture over the top of the frozen pie. Sprinkle with the chocolate and return to the freezer for 1½ hours or until firm. Serve at room temperature.

1

2

4

Crunchy Rhubarb Crumble

INGREDIENTS

Serves 6

125 g/4 oz plain flour
50 g/2 oz softened butter
50 g/2 oz rolled oats
50 g/2 oz demerara sugar
1 tbsp sesame seeds
½ tsp ground cinnamon
450 g/1 lb fresh rhubarb
50 g/2 oz caster sugar
custard or cream, to serve

TASTY TIP

To make homemade custard, pour 600 ml/1 pint of milk with a few drops of vanilla essence into a saucepan and bring to the boil. Remove from the heat and allow to cool. Meanwhile, whisk 5 egg yolks and 3 tablespoons of caster sugar together in a mixing bowl until thick and pale in colour. Add the milk, stir and strain into a heavy based saucepan. Cook the custard on a low heat, stirring constantly until the consistency of double cream. Pour over the rhubarb crumble and serve.

1 Preheat the oven to 180°C/350°F/Gas Mark 4. Place the flour in a large bowl and cut the butter into cubes. Add to the flour and rub in with the fingertips until the mixture resembles fine breadcrumbs, or blend for a few seconds in a food processor.

2 Stir in the rolled oats, demerara sugar, sesame seeds and cinnamon. Mix well and reserve.

3 Prepare the rhubarb by removing the thick ends of the stalks and cut diagonally into 2.5 cm/1 inch chunks. Wash thoroughly and pat dry with a clean tea towel. Place the rhubarb in a 1.1 litre/2 pint pie dish.

4 Sprinkle the caster sugar over the rhubarb and top with the reserved crumble mixture. Level the top of the crumble so that all the fruit is well covered and press down firmly. If liked, sprinkle the top with a little extra caster sugar.

5 Place on a baking sheet and bake in the preheated oven for 40–50 minutes, or until the fruit is soft and the topping is golden brown. Sprinkle the pudding with some more caster sugar and serve hot with custard or cream.

Lattice Treacle Tart

INGREDIENTS

Serves 4

For the pastry:
175 g/6 oz plain flour
40 g/1½ oz butter
40 g/1½ oz white vegetable fat

For the filling:
225 g/8 oz golden syrup
finely grated rind and juice of 1 lemon
75 g/3 oz fresh white breadcrumbs
1 small egg, beaten

1 Preheat the oven to 190°C/375°F/Gas Mark 5. Make the pastry by placing the flour, butter and white vegetable fat in a food processor. Blend in short sharp bursts until the mixture resembles fine breadcrumbs. Remove from the processor and place onto a pastry board or into a large bowl.

2 Stir in enough cold water to make a dough and knead in a large bowl or on a floured surface until smooth and pliable.

3 Roll out the pastry and use to line a 20.5 cm/8 inch loose-bottomed fluted flan dish or tin. Reserve the pastry trimmings for decoration. Chill for 30 minutes.

4 Meanwhile, to make the filling, place the golden syrup in a saucepan and warm gently with the lemon rind and juice. Tip the breadcrumbs into the pastry case and pour the syrup mixture over the top.

5 Roll the pastry trimmings out onto a lightly floured surface and cut into 6–8 thin strips. Lightly dampen the pastry edge of the tart, then place the strips across the filling in a lattice pattern. Brush the ends of the strips with water and seal to the edge of the tart. Brush a little beaten egg over the pastry and bake in the preheated oven for 25 minutes, or until the filling is just set. Serve hot or cold.

TASTY TIP
Why not replace the breadcrumbs with the same amount of desiccated coconut?

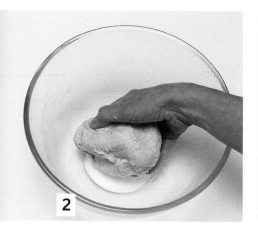
2

4

5

Chocolate Fruit Pizza

INGREDIENTS

Serves 8

1 quantity Sweet Shortcrust Pastry
 (see page 56)
2 tbsp chocolate spread
1 small peach, very thinly sliced
1 small nectarine, very thinly sliced
150 g/5 oz strawberries, halved
 or quartered
75 g/3 oz raspberries
75 g/3 oz blueberries
75 g/3 oz plain dark chocolate,
 coarsely chopped
1 tbsp butter, melted
2 tbsp sugar
75 g/3 oz white chocolate, chopped
1 tbsp hazelnuts, toasted
 and chopped
sprigs of fresh mint, to decorate

HELPFUL HINT

Alternatively, preheat the grill and grill the pizza until the fruits begin to caramelise and the white chocolate begins to melt, do not overheat as the white chocolate could split and become gritty.

1 Preheat the oven to 200°C/400°F/Gas Mark 6, 15 minutes before baking. Lightly oil a large baking sheet. Roll the prepared pastry out to a 23 cm/9 inch round and place the pastry round onto the baking sheet, and crimp the edges. Using a fork, prick the base all over and chill in the refrigerator for 30 minutes.

2 Line the pastry with tinfoil and weigh down with an ovenproof flat dinner plate or base of a large flan tin and bake blind in the preheated oven until the edges begin to colour. Remove from the oven and discard the weight and tinfoil.

3 Carefully spread the chocolate spread over the pizza base and arrange the peach and nectarine slices around the outside edge in overlapping circles. Toss the berries with the plain chocolate and arrange in the centre. Drizzle with the melted butter and sprinkle with the sugar.

4 Bake in the preheated oven for 10–12 minutes, or until the fruit begins to soften. Transfer the pizza to a wire rack.

5 Sprinkle the white chocolate and hazelnuts over the surface and return to the oven for 1 minute or until the chocolate begins to soften. If the pastry starts to darken too much, cover the edge with strips of tinfoil. Remove to a wire rack and leave to cool. Decorate with sprigs of fresh mint and serve warm.

1

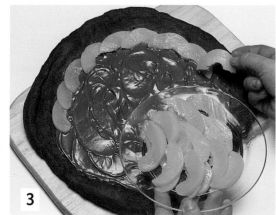

3

3

Sweet-stewed Dried Fruits

INGREDIENTS

Serves 4

500 g/1 lb 2 oz packet mixed dried
  fruit salad
450 ml/³/₄ pint apple juice
2 tbsp clear honey
2 tbsp brandy
1 lemon
1 orange

To decorate:
half-fat crème fraîche
fine strips of pared orange rind

1   Place the fruits, apple juice, clear honey and brandy in a small saucepan.

2   Using a small, sharp knife or a zester, carefully remove the zest from the lemon and orange and place in the pan.

3   Squeeze the juice from the lemon and orange and add to the pan.

4   Bring the fruit mixture to the boil and simmer for about 1 minute. Remove the pan from the heat and allow the mixture to cool completely.

5   Transfer the mixture to a large bowl, cover with clingfilm and chill in the refrigerator overnight to allow the flavours to blend.

6   Spoon the stewed fruit in 4 shallow dessert dishes. Decorate with a large spoonful of half-fat crème fraîche and a few strips of the pared orange rind and serve.

TASTY TIP

As a dessert, this dish is particularly good when served with cold rice pudding. However, these stewed fruits can also be very nice for breakfast. Simply pour some unsweetened muesli into the bottom of a bowl, top with the stewed fruits and perhaps some low-fat natural yogurt and serve.

Fruity Chocolate Bread Pudding

INGREDIENTS

Serves 4

175 g/6 oz plain dark chocolate
1 small fruit loaf
125 g/4 oz ready-to-eat dried apricots,
  roughly chopped
450 ml/¾ pint single cream
300 ml/½ pint milk
1 tbsp caster sugar
3 medium eggs
3 tbsp demerara sugar, for sprinkling

1 Preheat the oven to 180°C/350°F/Gas Mark 4, 10 minutes before cooking. Lightly butter a shallow ovenproof dish. Break the chocolate into small pieces, then place in a heatproof bowl set over a saucepan of gently simmering water. Heat gently, stirring frequently, until the chocolate has melted and is smooth. Remove from the heat and leave for about 10 minutes or until the chocolate begins to thicken slightly.

2 Cut the fruit loaf into medium to thick slices, then spread with the melted chocolate. Leave until almost set, then cut each slice in half to form a triangle. Layer the chocolate-coated bread slices and the chopped apricots in the buttered ovenproof dish.

3 Stir the cream and the milk together, then stir in the caster sugar. Beat the eggs, then gradually beat into the cream and milk mixture. Beat thoroughly until well blended. Carefully pour over the bread slices and apricots and leave to stand for 30 minutes.

4 Sprinkle with the demerara sugar and place in a roasting tin half filled with boiling water. Cook in the preheated oven for 45 minutes, or until golden and the custard is lightly set. Serve immediately.

HELPFUL HINT

It is important to leave the pudding to stand for at least 30 minutes, as described in step 3. This allows the custard to soak into the bread – otherwise it sets around the bread as it cooks, making the pudding seem stodgy.

2

3

4

Chocolate & Fruit Crumble

INGREDIENTS

Serves 4

For the crumble:

125 g/4 oz plain flour
125 g/4 oz butter
75 g/3 oz light soft brown sugar
50 g/2 oz rolled porridge oats
50 g/2 oz hazelnuts, chopped

For the filling:

450 g/1 lb Bramley apples
1 tbsp lemon juice
50 g/2 oz sultanas
50 g/2 oz seedless raisins
50 g/2 oz light soft brown sugar
350 g/12 oz pears, peeled,
   cored and chopped
1 tsp ground cinnamon
125 g/4 oz plain dark chocolate, very
   roughly chopped
2 tsp caster sugar for sprinkling

TASTY TIP

Bramley apples are ideal for cooking and will form a purée very easily. If you prefer, use a dessert apple such as Golden Delicious or Granny Smith, but reduce the sugar accordingly.

1 Preheat the oven to 190°C/375°F/Gas Mark 5, 10 minutes before baking. Lightly oil an ovenproof dish.

2 For the crumble, sift the flour into a large bowl. Cut the butter into small dice and add to the flour. Rub the butter into the flour until the mixture resembles fine breadcrumbs.

3 Stir the sugar, porridge oats and the chopped hazelnuts into the mixture and reserve.

4 For the filling, peel the apples, core and slice thickly. Place in a large heavy based saucepan with the lemon juice and 3 tablespoons of water. Add the sultanas, raisins and the soft brown sugar. Bring slowly to the boil, cover and simmer over a gentle heat for 8–10 minutes, stirring occasionally, or until the apples are slightly softened.

5 Remove the saucepan from the heat and leave to cool slightly before stirring in the pears, ground cinnamon and the chopped chocolate.

6 Spoon into the prepared ovenproof dish. Sprinkle the crumble evenly over the top then bake in the preheated oven for 35–40 minutes or until the top is golden. Remove from the oven, sprinkle with the caster sugar and serve immediately.

3

5

6

Osborne Pudding

INGREDIENTS

Serves 4

8 slices of white bread
50 g/2 oz butter
2 tbsp marmalade
50 g/2 oz luxury mixed dried fruit
2 tbsp fresh orange juice
40 g/1½ oz caster sugar
2 large eggs
450 ml/¾ pint milk
150 ml/¼ pint whipping cream

For the marmalade sauce:

zest and juice of 1 orange
2 tbsp thick-cut orange marmalade
1 tbsp brandy (optional)
2 tsp cornflour

TASTY TIP

To make an orange sauce instead, omit the marmalade and add the juice of another 3 oranges and a squeeze of lemon juice to make 250 ml/9 fl oz. Follow the recipe as before but increase the cornflour to 1½ tablespoons.

1   Preheat the oven to 170°C/325°F/Gas Mark 3. Lightly oil a 1.1 litre/ 2 pint baking dish.

2   Remove the crusts from the bread and spread thickly with the butter and marmalade. Cut the bread into small triangles.

3   Place half the bread in the base of the dish and sprinkle over the dried mixed fruit, 1 tablespoon of the orange juice and half the caster sugar.

4   Top with the remaining bread and marmalade, buttered side up and pour over the remaining orange juice. Sprinkle over the remaining caster sugar.

5   Whisk the eggs with the milk and cream and pour over the pudding. Reserve for about 30 minutes to allow the bread to absorb the liquid.

6   Place in a roasting tin and pour in enough boiling water to come halfway up the sides of the dish. Bake in the preheated oven for 50–60 minutes, or until the pudding is set and the top is crisp and golden.

7   Meanwhile, make the marmalade sauce. Heat the orange zest and juice with the marmalade and brandy if using.

8   Mix 1 tablespoon of water with the cornflour and mix together well.

9   Add to the saucepan and cook on a low heat, stirring until warmed through and thickened. Serve the pudding hot with the marmalade sauce.

2

3

5

Mocha Pie

INGREDIENTS

Serves 4–6

1 x 23 cm/9 inch ready-made sweet
   pastry case

For the filling:
125 g/4 oz plain dark chocolate,
   broken into pieces
175 g/6 oz unsalted butter
225 g/8 oz soft brown sugar
1 tsp vanilla essence
3 tbsp strong black coffee

For the topping:
600 ml/1 pint double cream
50 g/2 oz icing sugar
2 tsp vanilla essence
1 tsp instant coffee dissolved in
   1 tsp boiling water and cooled
grated plain and white chocolate,
   to decorate

1   Place the prepared pastry case onto a large serving plate and
    reserve. Melt the chocolate in a heatproof bowl set over a saucepan
    of simmering water. Ensure the water is not touching the base of
    the bowl. Remove from the heat, stir until smooth and leave to cool.

2   Cream the butter, soft brown sugar and vanilla essence until light
    and fluffy, then beat in the cooled chocolate. Add the strong black
    coffee, pour into the pastry case and chill in the refrigerator for
    about 30 minutes.

3   For the topping, whisk the cream until beginning to thicken, then
    whisk in the sugar and vanilla essence. Continue to whisk until the
    cream is softly peaking. Spoon just under half of the cream into
    a separate bowl and fold in the dissolved coffee.

4   Spread the remaining cream over the filling in the pastry case.
    Spoon the coffee-flavoured whipped cream evenly over the top,
    then swirl it decoratively with a palate knife. Sprinkle with grated
    chocolate and chill in the refrigerator until ready to serve.

HELPFUL HINT
Using a ready-made pastry
case makes this a quickly
made store cupboard pie that
looks very impressive.

2

3

4

Spicy White Chocolate Mousse

INGREDIENTS

Serves 4–6

6 cardamom pods
125 ml/4 fl oz milk
3 bay leaves
200 g/7 oz white chocolate
300 ml/½ pint double cream
3 medium egg whites
1–2 tsp cocoa powder, sifted,
  for dusting

1 Tap the cardamom pods lightly so they split. Remove the seeds, then, using a pestle and mortar, crush lightly. Pour the milk into a small saucepan and add the crushed seeds and the bay leaves. Bring to the boil gently over a medium heat. Remove from the heat, cover and leave in a warm place for at least 30 minutes to infuse.

2 Break the chocolate into small pieces and place in a heatproof bowl set over a saucepan of gently simmering water. Ensure the water is not touching the base of the bowl. When the chocolate has melted remove the bowl from the heat and stir until smooth.

3 Whip the cream until it has slightly thickened and holds its shape, but does not form peaks. Reserve. Whisk the egg whites in a clean, grease-free bowl until stiff and standing in soft peaks.

4 Strain the milk through a sieve into the cooled, melted chocolate and beat until smooth. Spoon the chocolate mixture into the egg whites, then using a large metal spoon, fold gently. Add the whipped cream and fold in gently.

5 Spoon into a large serving dish or individual small cups. Chill in the refrigerator for 3–4 hours. Just before serving, dust with a little sifted cocoa powder and then serve.

TASTY TIP

Chocolate and spices go together very well as this recipe demonstrates. White chocolate has an affinity with spices such as cardamom, while dark and milk chocolate go very well with cinnamon.

2

3

4

Entertaining

Now that you have mastered the basics try these simple-to-follow yet sophisticated dishes that will amaze your guests. The range of recipes helps you to cater for every occasion and for whatever your guests need with nibbles, fish courses, vegetarian and meat dishes.

Mixed Canapés

INGREDIENTS

Serves 12

For the stir-fried cheese canapés:
6 thick slices white bread

40 g/1½ oz butter, softened

75 g/3 oz mature Cheddar
cheese, grated

75 g/3 oz blue cheese such as Stilton
or Gorgonzola, crumbled

3 tbsp sunflower oil

For the spicy nuts:
25 g/1 oz unsalted butter

2 tbsp light olive oil

450 g/1 lb mixed unsalted nuts

1 tsp ground paprika

½ tsp ground cumin

½ tsp fine sea salt

sprigs of fresh coriander, to garnish

TASTY TIP

These canapés are perfect for serving at a buffet or finger food party, or you can halve the quantities and serve with drinks instead of a starter at an informal dinner party for 4–6 people.

1   For the cheese canapés, cut the crusts off the bread, then gently roll with a rolling pin to flatten slightly. Thinly spread with butter, then sprinkle over the mixed cheeses as evenly as possible.

2   Roll up each slice tightly, then cut into 4 slices, each about 2.5 cm/ 1 inch long. Heat the oil in a wok or large frying pan and stir-fry the cheese rolls in 2 batches, turning them all the time until golden brown and crisp. Drain on absorbent kitchen paper and serve warm or cold.

3   For the spicy nuts, melt the butter and oil in a wok, then add the nuts and stir-fry over a low heat for about 5 minutes, stirring all the time, or until they begin to colour.

4   Sprinkle the paprika and cumin over the nuts and continue stir-frying for a further 1–2 minutes, or until the nuts are golden brown.

5   Remove from the wok and drain on absorbent kitchen paper. Sprinkle with the salt, garnish with sprigs of fresh coriander and serve hot or cold. If serving cold, store both the cheese canapés and the spicy nuts in airtight containers.

Thai Crab Cakes

INGREDIENTS

Serves 6

225 g/8 oz white and brown crabmeat
  (about equivalent to the flesh of
  2 medium crabs)
1 tsp ground coriander
¼ tsp chilli powder
¼ tsp ground turmeric
2 tsp lime juice
1 tsp soft light brown sugar
2.5 cm/1 inch piece fresh root ginger,
  peeled and grated
3 tbsp freshly chopped coriander
2 tsp finely chopped lemon grass
2 tbsp plain flour
2 medium eggs, separated
50 g/2 oz fresh white breadcrumbs
3 tbsp groundnut oil
lime wedges, to garnish
mixed salad leaves, to serve

1 Place the crabmeat in a bowl with the ground coriander, chilli, turmeric, lime juice, sugar, ginger, chopped coriander, lemon grass, flour and egg yolks. Mix together well.

2 Divide the mixture into 12 equal portions and form each into a small patty about 5 cm/2 inches across. Lightly whisk the egg whites and put into a dish. Place the breadcrumbs onto a separate plate.

3 Dip each crab cake, first in the egg whites, then in the breadcrumbs, turning to coat both sides. Place on a plate, cover and chill in the refrigerator until ready to cook.

4 Heat the oil in a large frying pan. Add 6 crab cakes and cook for 3 minutes on each side, or until crisp and golden brown on the outside and cooked through. Remove, drain on absorbent kitchen paper and keep warm while cooking the remaining cakes. Arrange on plates, garnish with lime wedges and serve immediately with salad leaves.

1

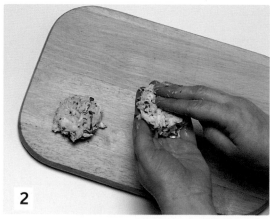

2

3

Sesame Prawn Toasts

INGREDIENTS

Serves 4

125 g/4 oz peeled cooked prawns
1 tbsp cornflour
2 spring onions, peeled and
  roughly chopped
2 tsp freshly grated root ginger
2 tsp dark soy sauce
pinch of Chinese five-spice
  powder (optional)
1 small egg, beaten
salt and freshly ground black pepper
6 thin slices day-old white bread
40 g/1½ oz sesame seeds
vegetable oil for deep-frying
chilli sauce, to serve

HELPFUL HINT

The toasts can be prepared to the end of step 3 up to 12 hours in advance. Cover and chill in the refrigerator until needed. It is important to use bread that is a day or two old and not fresh bread. Make sure that the prawns are well-drained before puréeing – pat them dry on absorbent kitchen paper, if necessary.

1 Place the prawns in a food processor or blender with the cornflour, spring onions, ginger, soy sauce and Chinese-five spice powder, if using. Blend to a fairly smooth paste. Spoon into a bowl and stir in the beaten egg. Season to taste with salt and pepper.

2 Cut the crusts off the bread. Spread the prawn paste in an even layer on one side of each slice. Sprinkle over the sesame seeds and press down lightly.

3 Cut each slice diagonally into 4 triangles. Place on a board and chill in the refrigerator for 30 minutes.

4 Pour sufficient oil into a heavy based saucepan or deep-fat fryer so that it is one-third full. Heat until it reaches a temperature of 180°C/350°F. Cook the toasts in batches of 5 or 6, carefully lowering them seeded-side down into the oil. Deep-fry for 2–3 minutes, or until lightly browned, then turn over and cook for 1 minute more. Using a slotted spoon, lift out the toasts and drain on absorbent kitchen paper. Keep warm while frying the remaining toasts. Arrange on a warmed platter and serve immediately with some chilli sauce for dipping.

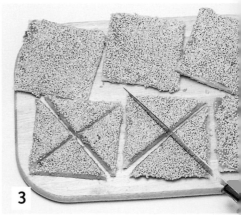

Cooked Vegetable Salad with Satay Sauce

INGREDIENTS

Serves 4

125 ml/4 fl oz groundnut oil
225 g/8 oz unsalted peanuts
1 onion, peeled and finely chopped
1 garlic clove, peeled and crushed
½ tsp chilli powder
1 tsp ground coriander
½ tsp ground cumin
½ tsp sugar
1 tbsp dark soy sauce
2 tbsp fresh lemon juice
2 tbsp light olive oil
salt and freshly ground black pepper
125 g/4 oz French green beans,
   trimmed and halved
125 g/4 oz carrots
125 g/4 oz cauliflower florets
125 g/4 oz broccoli florets
125 g/4 oz Chinese leaves or pak
   choi, trimmed and shredded
125 g/4 oz beansprouts
1 tbsp sesame oil

To garnish:
sprigs of fresh watercress
cucumber, cut into slivers

1 Heat a wok, add the oil, and when hot, add the peanuts and stir-fry for 3–4 minutes. Drain on absorbent kitchen paper and leave to cool. Blend in a food processor to a fine powder.

2 Place the onion and garlic, with the spices, sugar, soy sauce, lemon juice and olive oil in a food processor. Season to taste with salt and pepper, then process into a paste. Transfer to a wok and stir-fry for 3–4 minutes.

3 Stir 600 ml/1 pint hot water into the paste and bring to the boil. Add the ground peanuts and simmer gently for 5–6 minutes or until the mixture thickens. Reserve the satay sauce.

4 Cook in batches in lightly salted boiling water. Cook the French beans, carrots, cauliflower and broccoli for 3–4 minutes, and the Chinese leaves or pak choi and beansprouts for 2 minutes. Drain each batch, drizzle over the sesame oil and arrange on a large warmed serving dish. Garnish with watercress sprigs and cucumber. Serve with the satay sauce.

1

2

3

Spicy Prawns in Lettuce Cups

INGREDIENTS

Serves 4

1 lemon grass stalk
225 g/8 oz peeled cooked prawns
1 tsp finely grated lime zest
1 red bird's-eye chilli, deseeded and
  finely chopped
2.5 cm/1 inch piece fresh root ginger,
  peeled and grated
2 Little Gem lettuces, divided
  into leaves
25 g/1 oz roasted peanuts, chopped
2 spring onions, trimmed and
  diagonally sliced
sprig of fresh coriander, to garnish

For the coconut sauce:

2 tbsp freshly grated or unsweetened
  shredded coconut
1 tbsp hoisin sauce
1 tbsp light soy sauce
1 tbsp Thai fish sauce
1 tbsp palm sugar or soft light
  brown sugar

1 Remove 3 or 4 of the tougher outer leaves of the lemon grass and reserve for another dish. Finely chop the remaining softer centre. Place 2 teaspoons of the chopped lemon grass in a bowl with the prawns, grated lime zest, chilli and ginger. Mix together to coat the prawns. Cover and place in the refrigerator to marinate while you make the coconut sauce.

2 For the sauce, place the grated coconut in a wok or nonstick frying pan and dry-fry for 2–3 minutes or until golden. Remove from the pan and reserve. Add the hoisin, soy and fish sauces to the pan with the sugar and 4 tablespoons of water. Simmer for 2–3 minutes, then remove from the heat. Leave to cool.

3 Pour the sauce over the prawns, add the toasted coconut and toss to mix together. Divide the prawn and coconut sauce mixture between the lettuce leaves and arrange on a platter.

4 Sprinkle over the chopped roasted peanuts and spring onions and garnish with a sprig of fresh coriander. Serve immediately.

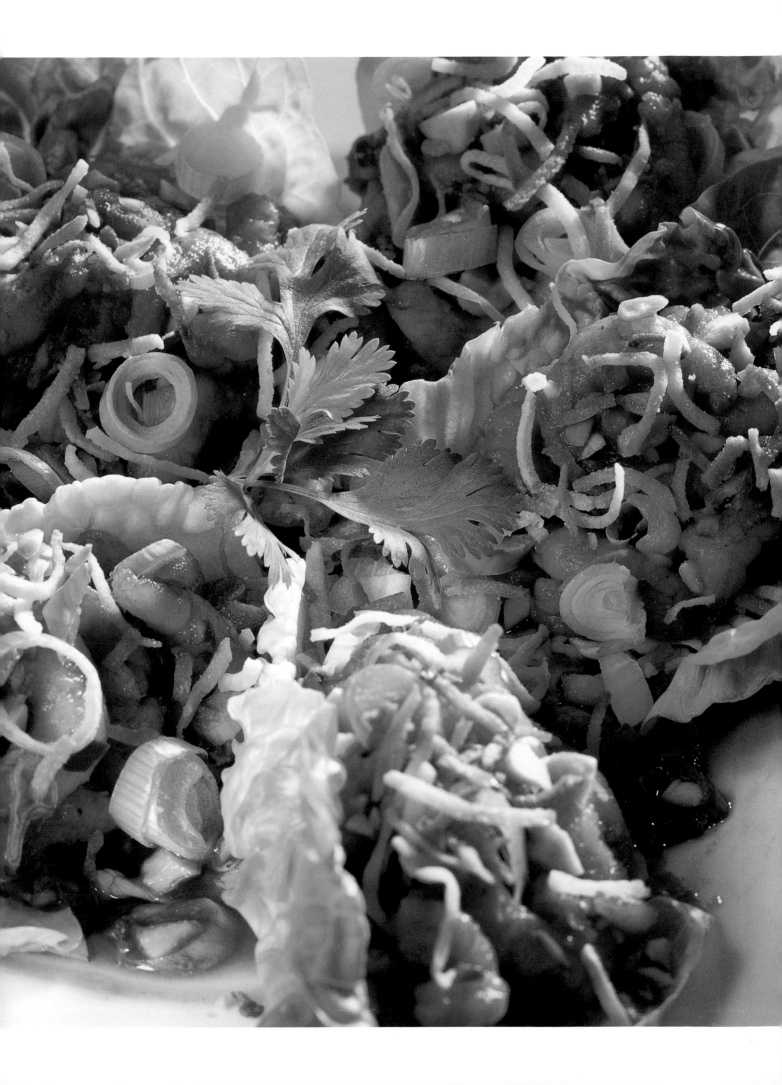

Barbecued Fish Kebabs

INGREDIENTS

Serves 4

450 g/1 lb herring or mackerel fillets, cut into chunks
2 small red onions, peeled and quartered
16 cherry tomatoes
salt and freshly ground black pepper

For the sauce:

150 ml/¼ pint fish stock
5 tbsp tomato ketchup
2 tbsp Worcestershire sauce
2 tbsp wine vinegar
2 tbsp brown sugar
2 drops Tabasco
2 tbsp tomato purée

TASTY TIP

Instead of cooking indoors, cook these kebabs on the barbecue for a delicious charcoaled flavour. Light the barbecue at least 20 minutes before use in order to allow the coals to heat up. Barbecue some peppers and red onions and serve with a mixed salad as an accompaniment to the fish kebabs.

1 Line a grill rack with a single layer of tinfoil and preheat the grill at a high temperature, 2 minutes before use.

2 If using wooden skewers, soak in cold water for 30 minutes to prevent them from catching alight during cooking.

3 Meanwhile, prepare the sauce. Add the fish stock, tomato ketchup, Worcestershire sauce, vinegar, sugar, Tabasco and tomato purée to a small saucepan. Stir well and leave to simmer for 5 minutes.

4 When ready to cook, drain the skewers, if necessary, then thread the fish chunks, the quartered red onions and the cherry tomatoes alternately onto the skewers.

5 Season the kebabs to taste with salt and pepper and brush with the sauce. Grill under the preheated grill for 8–10 minutes, basting with the sauce occasionally during cooking. Turn the kebabs often to ensure that they are cooked thoroughly and evenly on all sides. Serve immediately with couscous.

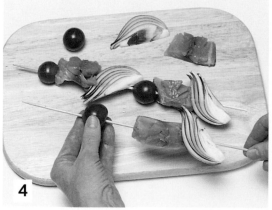

Fish Puff Tart

INGREDIENTS

Serves 4

350 g/12 oz prepared puff
  pastry, thawed if frozen
150 g/5 oz smoked haddock
150 g/5 oz cod
1 tbsp pesto sauce
2 tomatoes, sliced
125 g/4 oz goats' cheese, sliced
1 medium egg, beaten
freshly chopped parsley, to garnish

FOOD FACT

The Scottish name for smoked haddock is finnan haddie, named after the Scottish fishing village of Findon near Aberdeen. Smoked haddock has been a favourite breakfast dish in Findon and the rest of Scotland for many years. Although this type of fish was traditionally caught and smoked (sometimes over peat fires) in Scotland, nowadays the fish is produced in New England and other eastern coastal states of the United States.

1. Preheat the oven to 220°C/425°F/Gas Mark 7. On a lightly floured surface roll out the pastry into a 20.5 x 25.5 cm/ 8 x 10 inch rectangle.

2. Draw a 18 x 23 cm/7 x 9 inch rectangle in the centre of the pastry, to form a 2.5 cm/1 inch border. (Be careful not to cut through the pastry.)

3. Lightly cut criss-cross patterns in the border of the pastry with a knife.

4. Place the fish on a chopping board and with a sharp knife skin the cod and smoked haddock. Cut into thin slices.

5. Spread the pesto evenly over the bottom of the pastry case with the back of a spoon.

6. Arrange the fish, tomatoes and cheese in the pastry case and brush the pastry with the beaten egg.

7. Bake the tart in the preheated oven for 20–25 minutes, until the pastry is well risen, puffed and golden brown. Garnish with the chopped parsley and serve immediately.

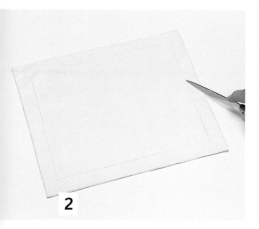

2

4

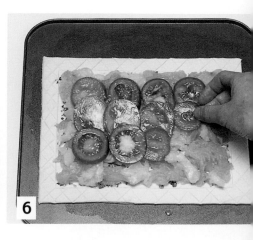

6

Chicken & New Potatoes on Rosemary Skewers

INGREDIENTS

Serves 4

8 thick fresh rosemary stems, at least
   23 cm/9 inches long

3–4 tbsp extra-virgin olive oil

2 garlic cloves, peeled and crushed

1 tsp freshly chopped thyme

grated rind and juice of 1 lemon

salt and freshly ground black pepper

4 skinless chicken breast fillets

16 small new potatoes, peeled
   or scrubbed

8 very small onions or
   shallots, peeled

1 large yellow or red
   pepper, deseeded

lemon wedges, to garnish

parsley-flavoured cooked rice,
   to serve

1 Preheat the grill and line the grill rack with tinfoil just before cooking. If using a barbecue, light at least 20 minutes before required. Strip the leaves from the rosemary stems, leaving about 5 cm/2 inches of soft leaves at the top. Chop the leaves coarsely and reserve. Using a sharp knife, cut the thicker woody ends of the stems to a point which can pierce the chicken pieces and potatoes. Blend the chopped rosemary, oil, garlic, thyme and lemon rind and juice in a shallow dish. Season to taste with salt and pepper.

2 Cut the chicken into 4 cm/1½ inch cubes, add to the flavoured oil and stir well. Cover, refrigerate for at least 30 minutes, turning occasionally.

3 Cook the potatoes in lightly salted boiling water for 10–12 minutes until just tender. Add the onions to the potatoes 2 minutes before the end of the cooking time. Drain, rinse under cold running water and leave to cool. Cut the pepper into 2.5 cm/1 inch squares.

4 Beginning with a piece of chicken and starting with the pointed end of the skewer, alternately thread equal amounts of chicken, potato, pepper and onion onto each rosemary skewer. Cover the leafy ends of the skewers with tinfoil to stop them from burning. Do not thread the chicken and vegetables too closely together on the skewer or the chicken may not cook completely.

5 Cook the kebabs for 15 minutes, or until tender and golden, turning and brushing with either extra oil or the marinade. Remove the tinfoil, garnish with lemon wedges and serve on rice.

1

4

5

Sweet-&-Sour Rice with Chicken

INGREDIENTS

Serves 4

4 spring onions

2 tsp sesame oil

1 tsp Chinese five-spice powder

450 g/1 lb chicken breast,
  cut into cubes

1 tbsp oil

1 garlic clove, peeled and crushed

1 medium onion, peeled and sliced
  into thin wedges

225 g/8 oz long-grain white rice

600 ml/1 pint water

4 tbsp tomato ketchup

1 tbsp tomato purée

2 tbsp honey

1 tbsp vinegar

1 tbsp dark soy sauce

1 carrot, peeled and cut
  into matchsticks

FOOD FACT

Five-spice powder is a popular Chinese seasoning that can be bought ready-blended in jars. It is a mixture of finely ground star anise, fennel, cinnamon, cloves and Sichuan pepper and adds a unique aniseed flavour to food.

1 Trim the spring onions, then cut lengthways into fine strips. Drop into a large bowl of iced water and reserve.

2 Mix together the sesame oil and Chinese five-spice powder and use to rub into the cubed chicken. Heat the wok, then add the oil and when hot, cook the garlic and onion for 2–3 minutes, or until transparent and softened.

3 Add the chicken and stir-fry over a medium-high heat until the chicken is golden and cooked through. Using a slotted spoon, remove from the wok and keep warm.

4 Stir the rice into the wok and add the water, tomato ketchup, tomato purée, honey, vinegar and soy sauce. Stir well to mix. Bring to the boil, then simmer until almost all of the liquid is absorbed. Stir in the carrot and reserved chicken and continue to cook for 3–4 minutes.

5 Drain the spring onions, which will have become curly. Garnish with the spring onion curls and serve immediately with the rice and chicken.

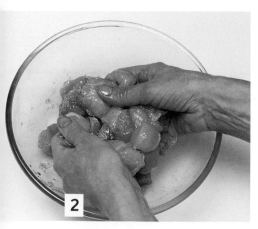

Turkey & Pesto Rice Roulades

INGREDIENTS

Serves 4

125 g/4 oz cooked white rice, at
   room temperature
1 garlic clove, peeled and crushed
1–2 tbsp Parmesan cheese, grated
2 tbsp prepared pesto sauce
2 tbsp pine nuts, lightly toasted
   and chopped
4 turkey steaks, each weighing
   about 150 g/5 oz
salt and freshly ground black pepper
4 slices Parma ham
2 tbsp olive oil
50 ml/2 fl oz white wine
25 g/1 oz unsalted butter, chilled

To serve:
freshly cooked spinach
freshly cooked pasta

FOOD FACT
The classic Italian Parma ham is
dry-cured, whereby it is rubbed
with salt for about a month, then
hung up to dry for a year. Carved
very thinly, it often served raw, but
is also good when lightly fried.

1 Put the rice in a bowl and add the garlic, Parmesan cheese, pesto and pine nuts. Stir to combine the ingredients, then reserve.

2 Place the turkey steaks on a chopping board and, using a sharp knife, cut horizontally through each steak, without cutting right through. Open up the steaks and cover with baking parchment. Flatten slightly by pounding with a meat mallet or rolling pin.

3 Season each steak with salt and pepper. Divide the stuffing equally among the steaks, spreading evenly over one half. Fold the steaks in half to enclose the filling, then wrap each steak in a slice of Parma ham and secure with cocktail sticks.

4 Heat the oil in a large frying pan over medium heat. Cook the steaks for 5 minutes, or until golden on one side. Turn and cook for a further 2 minutes. Push the steaks to the side and pour in the wine. Allow the wine to bubble and evaporate. Add the butter, a little at a time, whisking constantly until the sauce is smooth. Discard the cocktail sticks, then serve the steaks drizzled with the sauce and serve with spinach and pasta.

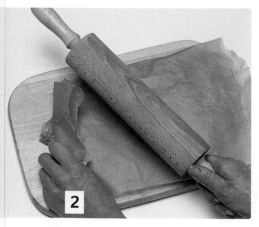

2

3

4

Shredded Duck in Lettuce Leaves

INGREDIENTS

Serves 4–6

15 g/½ oz dried Chinese
  (shiitake) mushrooms
2 tbsp vegetable oil
400 g/14 oz boneless, skinless
  duck breast, cut crossways into
  thin strips
1 red chilli, deseeded and diagonally
  thinly sliced
4–6 spring onions, trimmed and
  diagonally sliced
2 garlic cloves, peeled and crushed
75 g/3 oz beansprouts
3 tbsp soy sauce
1 tbsp Chinese rice wine or dry sherry
1–2 tsp clear honey or brown sugar
4–6 tbsp hoisin sauce
large, crisp lettuce leaves such as
  iceberg or cos
handful of fresh mint leaves
dipping sauce, to serve

1   Cover the dried Chinese mushrooms with almost boiling water, leave for 20 minutes, then drain and slice thinly.

2   Heat a large wok, add the oil and when hot stir-fry the duck for 3–4 minutes, or until sealed. Remove with a slotted spoon and reserve.

3   Add the chilli, spring onions, garlic and Chinese mushrooms to the wok and stir-fry for 2–3 minutes, or until softened.

4   Add the beansprouts, soy sauce, Chinese rice wine or dry sherry and honey or brown sugar to the wok, and continue to stir-fry for 1 minute, or until blended.

5   Stir in the reserved duck and stir-fry for 2 minutes, or until well mixed together and heated right through. Transfer to a heated serving dish.

6   Arrange the hoisin sauce in a small bowl on a tray or plate with a pile of lettuce leaves and the mint leaves.

7   Let each guest spoon a little hoisin sauce onto a lettuce leaf, then top with a large spoonful of the stir-fried duck and vegetables and roll up the leaf to enclose the filling. Serve with the dipping sauce.

FOOD FACT

Hoisin sauce is a sweet and spicy aromatic Chinese sauce made primarily from soy beans, sugar, garlic and chilli.

Rabbit Italian

INGREDIENTS

Serves 4

450 g/1 lb diced rabbit, thawed
  if frozen
6 rashers streaky bacon
1 garlic clove, peeled
1 onion, peeled
1 carrot, peeled
1 celery stalk
25 g/1 oz butter
2 tbsp olive oil
400 g can chopped tomatoes
150 ml/¼ pint red wine
salt and freshly ground black pepper
125 g/4 oz mushrooms

To serve:

freshly cooked pasta
green salad

1. Trim the rabbit if necessary. Chop the bacon and reserve. Chop the garlic and onion and slice the carrot thinly, then trim the celery and chop.

2. Heat the butter and 1 tablespoon of the oil in a large saucepan and brown the rabbit for 5 minutes, stirring frequently, until sealed all over. Transfer the rabbit to a plate and reserve.

3. Add the garlic, bacon, celery, carrot and onion to the saucepan and cook for a further 5 minutes, stirring occasionally, until softened, then return the rabbit to the saucepan and pour over the tomatoes with their juice and the wine. Season to taste with salt and pepper. Bring to the boil, cover, reduce the heat and simmer for 45 minutes.

4. Meanwhile, wipe the mushrooms and if large, cut in half. Heat the remaining oil in a small frying pan and sauté the mushrooms for 2 minutes. Drain, then add to the rabbit and cook for 15 minutes, or until the rabbit is tender. Season to taste and serve immediately with freshly cooked pasta and a green salad.

HELPFUL HINT

If you prefer to buy a whole rabbit, have your butcher joint it for you into 8 pieces. The method and cooking time will remain the same.

1

2

3

Pan-fried Beef with Creamy Mushrooms

INGREDIENTS

Serves 4

225 g/8 oz shallots, peeled
2 garlic cloves, peeled
2 tbsp olive oil
4 medallions of beef
4 plum tomatoes
125 g/4 oz flat mushrooms
3 tbsp brandy
150 ml/¼ pint red wine
salt and freshly ground black pepper
4 tbsp double cream

To serve:

baby new potatoes
freshly cooked green beans

1 Cut the shallots in half if large, then chop the garlic. Heat the oil in a large frying pan and cook the shallots for about 8 minutes, stirring occasionally, until almost softened. Add the garlic and beef and cook for 8–10 minutes, turning once during cooking until the meat is browned all over. Using a slotted spoon, transfer the beef to a plate and keep warm.

2 Rinse the tomatoes and cut into eighths, then wipe the mushrooms and slice. Add to the pan and cook for 5 minutes, stirring frequently until the mushrooms have softened.

3 Pour in the brandy and heat through. Draw the pan off the heat and carefully ignite. Allow the flames to subside. Pour in the wine, return to the heat and bring to the boil. Boil until reduced by one-third. Draw the pan off the heat, season to taste with salt and pepper, add the cream and stir.

4 Arrange the beef on serving plates and spoon over the sauce. Serve with baby new potatoes and a few green beans.

HELPFUL HINT

To prepare medallions of beef, buy a piece of fillet weighing approximately 700 g/1½ lb. Cut crosswise into 4 pieces.

Fillet Steaks with Tomato & Garlic Sauce

INGREDIENTS

Serves 4

700 g/1½ lb ripe tomatoes
2 garlic cloves
2 tbsp olive oil
2 tbsp freshly chopped basil
2 tbsp freshly chopped oregano
2 tbsp red wine
salt and freshly ground black pepper
75 g/3 oz pitted black olives, chopped
4 fillet steaks, about 175 g/6 oz each
   in weight
freshly cooked vegetables, to serve

1 Make a small cross on the top of each tomato and place in a large bowl. Cover with boiling water and leave for 2 minutes. Using a slotted spoon, remove the tomatoes and skin carefully. Repeat until all the tomatoes are skinned. Place on a chopping board, cut into quarters, remove the seeds and roughly chop, then reserve.

2 Peel and chop the garlic. Heat half the olive oil in a saucepan and cook the garlic for 30 seconds. Add the chopped tomatoes with the basil, oregano, red wine and season to taste with salt and pepper. Bring to the boil then reduce the heat, cover and simmer for 15 minutes, stirring occasionally, or until the sauce is reduced and thickened. Stir the olives into the sauce and keep warm while cooking the steaks.

3 Meanwhile, lightly oil a griddle pan or heavy based frying pan with the remaining olive oil and cook the steaks for 2 minutes on each side to seal. Continue to cook the steaks for a further 2–4 minutes, depending on personal preference. Serve the steaks immediately with the garlic sauce and freshly cooked vegetables.

HELPFUL HINT

Fillet steak should be a deep mahogany colour with a good marbling of fat. If the meat is bright red or if the fat is bright white the meat has not been aged properly and will probably be quite tough.

Chinese Beef with Angel Hair Pasta

INGREDIENTS

Serves 4

1 tbsp pink peppercorns

1 tbsp chilli powder

1 tbsp Szechuan pepper

3 tbsp light soy sauce

3 tbsp dry sherry

450 g/1 lb sirloin steak, cut
  into strips

350 g/12 oz angel hair pasta

1 tbsp sesame oil

1 tbsp sunflower oil

1 bunch spring onions, trimmed
  and finely shredded, plus extra
  to garnish

1 red pepper, deseeded and
  thinly sliced

1 green pepper, deseeded and
  thinly sliced

1 tbsp toasted sesame seeds,
  to garnish

FOOD FACT

Szechuan pepper is the reddish-
brown dried berry of the
Chinese prickly ash tree and
has a pronounced spicy, woody
flavour. It is one of the
essential ingredients of Chinese
five-spice powder.

1 Crush the peppercorns, using a pestle and mortar. Transfer to a shallow bowl and combine with the chilli powder, Szechuan pepper, light soy sauce and sherry. Add the beef strips and stir until lightly coated. Cover and place in the refrigerator to marinate for 3 hours; stir occasionally during this time.

2 When ready to cook, bring a large pan of lightly salted water to a rolling boil. Add the pasta and cook according to the packet instructions, or until 'al dente'. Drain thoroughly and return to the pan. Add the sesame oil and toss lightly. Keep the pasta warm.

3 Heat a wok or large frying pan, add the sunflower oil and heat until very hot. Add the shredded spring onions with the sliced red and green peppers and stir-fry for 2 minutes.

4 Drain the beef, reserving the marinade, then add the beef to the wok or pan and stir-fry for 3 minutes. Pour the marinade and stir-fry for 1–2 minutes, until the steak is tender.

5 Pile the pasta onto 4 warmed plates. Top with the stir-fried beef and peppers and garnish with toasted sesame seeds and shredded spring onions. Serve immediately.

1

3

4

Roasted Lamb with Rosemary & Garlic

INGREDIENTS

Serves 6

1.6 kg/3½ lb leg of lamb
8 garlic cloves, peeled
few sprigs of fresh rosemary
salt and freshly ground black pepper
4 slices pancetta
4 tbsp olive oil
4 tbsp red wine vinegar
900 g/2 lb potatoes
1 large onion
sprigs of fresh rosemary, to garnish
freshly cooked ratatouille, to serve

HELPFUL HINT

If you are unable to get a leg of lamb weighing exactly 1.6 kg/ 3½ lb, calculate the cooking time as follows: 20 minutes per 450 g/ 1 lb plus 30 minutes for rare, 25 minutes per 450 g/1 lb plus 30 minutes for medium and 30 minutes per 450 g/1 lb plus 30 minutes for well-done.

1 Preheat the oven to 200°C/400°F/Gas Mark 6, 15 minutes before roasting. Wipe the leg of lamb with a clean damp cloth, then place the lamb in a large roasting tin. With a sharp knife, make small, deep incisions into the meat. Cut 2–3 garlic cloves into small slivers, then insert with a few small sprigs of rosemary into the lamb. Season to taste with salt and pepper and cover the lamb with the slices of pancetta.

2 Drizzle over 1 tablespoon of the olive oil and lay a few more rosemary sprigs across the lamb. Roast in the preheated oven for 30 minutes, then pour over the vinegar.

3 Peel the potatoes and cut into large dice. Peel the onion and cut into thick wedges then thickly slice the remaining garlic. Arrange around the lamb. Pour the remaining olive oil over the potatoes, then reduce the oven temperature to 180°C/350°F/Gas Mark 4 and roast for a further 1 hour, or until the lamb is tender. Garnish with fresh sprigs of rosemary and serve immediately with the roast potatoes and ratatouille.

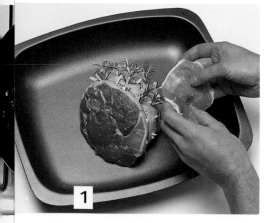

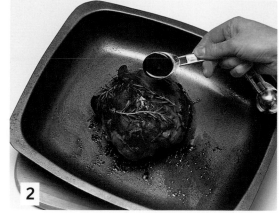

Marinated Lamb Chops with Garlic Fried Potatoes

INGREDIENTS

Serves 4

4 thick lamb chops
3 tbsp olive oil
550 g/1¼ lb potatoes, peeled and
   cut into 1 cm/½ inch dice
6 unpeeled garlic cloves
mixed salad or freshly cooked
   vegetables, to serve

For the marinade:

1 small bunch of fresh thyme,
   leaves removed
1 tbsp freshly chopped rosemary
1 tsp salt
2 garlic cloves, peeled and crushed
rind and juice of 1 lemon
2 tbsp olive oil

TASTY TIP

Marinating the chops not only adds flavour, but tenderises as well, due to the acids in the lemon juice. If time allows, marinate the chops for slightly longer. Try other citrus juices in this recipe for a change. Both orange and lime juice would be delicious.

1   Trim the chops of any excess fat, wipe with a clean damp cloth and reserve. To make the marinade, using a pestle and mortar, pound the thyme leaves and rosemary with the salt until pulpy. Add the garlic and continue pounding until crushed. Stir in the lemon rind and juice and the olive oil.

2   Pour the marinade over the lamb chops, turning them until they are well coated. Cover lightly and leave to marinate in the refrigerator for about 1 hour.

3   Meanwhile, heat the oil in a large non-stick frying pan. Add the potatoes and garlic and cook over a low heat for about 20 minutes, stirring occasionally. Increase the heat and cook for a further 10–15 minutes until golden. Drain on absorbent kitchen paper and add salt to taste. Keep warm.

4   Heat a griddle pan until almost smoking. Add the lamb chops and cook for 3–4 minutes on each side until golden, but still pink in the middle. Serve with the potatoes, and either a mixed salad or freshly cooked vegetables.

1

2

3

Lamb Pilaf

INGREDIENTS

Serves 4

2 tbsp vegetable oil

25 g/1 oz flaked or slivered almonds

1 medium onion, peeled and
finely chopped

1 medium carrot, peeled and
finely chopped

1 celery stalk, trimmed and
finely chopped

350 g/12 oz lean lamb, cut
into chunks

¼ tsp ground cinnamon

¼ tsp chilli flakes

2 large tomatoes, skinned, deseeded
and chopped

grated rind of 1 orange

350 g/12 oz easy-cook brown
basmati rice

600 ml/1 pint vegetable or
lamb stock

2 tbsp freshly snipped chives

3 tbsp freshly chopped coriander

salt and freshly ground black pepper

To garnish:

lemon slices

sprigs of fresh coriander

1 Preheat the oven to 140°C/275°F/Gas Mark 1. Heat the oil in a flameproof casserole dish with a tight-fitting lid and add the almonds. Cook for about 1 minute until just starting to brown, stirring often. Add the onion, carrot and celery and cook gently for a further 8–10 minutes until soft and lightly browned.

2 Increase the heat and add the lamb. Cook for a further 5 minutes until the lamb has changed colour. Add the ground cinnamon and chilli flakes and stir briefly before adding the tomatoes and orange rind.

3 Stir and add the rice, then the stock. Bring slowly to the boil and cover tightly. Transfer to the preheated oven and cook for 30–35 minutes until the rice is tender and the stock is absorbed.

4 Remove from the oven and leave to stand for 5 minutes before stirring in the chives and coriander. Season to taste with salt and pepper. Garnish with the lemon slices and sprigs of fresh coriander and serve immediately.

Antipasto Penne

INGREDIENTS

Serves 4

3 medium courgettes, trimmed

4 plum tomatoes

175 g/6 oz Italian ham

2 tbsp olive oil

salt and freshly ground black pepper

350 g/12 oz dried penne pasta

285 g jar antipasto

125 g/4 oz mozzarella cheese, drained
  and diced

125 g/4 oz Gorgonzola
  cheese, crumbled

3 tbsp freshly chopped
  flat-leaf parsley

FOOD FACT

The term antipasto refers to the course served before the pasto or meal begins and its purpose is to whet the appetite for the following courses. In Italy, these are served in small quantities, though 2 or 3 different dishes may be served at once. There are no hard and fast rules as to what constitutes a suitable dish for antipasti – there are literally thousands of regional variations.

1 Preheat the grill just before cooking. Cut the courgettes into thick slices. Rinse the tomatoes and cut into quarters, then cut the ham into strips. Pour the oil into a baking dish and place under the grill for 2 minutes, or until almost smoking. Remove from the grill and stir in the courgettes. Return to the grill and cook for 8 minutes, stirring occasionally. Remove from the grill and add the tomatoes and cook for a further 3 minutes.

2 Add the ham to the baking dish and cook under the grill for 4 minutes, until all the vegetables are charred and the ham is brown. Season to taste with salt and pepper.

3 Meanwhile, plunge the pasta into a large saucepan of lightly salted, boiling water, return to a rolling boil, stir and cook for 8 minutes, or until 'al dente'. Drain well and return to the saucepan.

4 Stir the antipasto into the vegetables and cook under the grill for 2 minutes, or until heated through. Add the cooked pasta and toss together gently with the remaining ingredients. Grill for a further 4 minutes, then serve immediately.

1

2

4

Jamaican Jerk Pork with Rice & Beans

INGREDIENTS

Serves 4

175 g/6 oz dried red kidney beans,
   soaked overnight
2 onions, peeled and chopped
2 garlic cloves, peeled and crushed
4 tbsp lime juice
2 tbsp each dark molasses, soy sauce
   and chopped fresh root ginger
2 jalapeño chillies, deseeded
   and chopped
½ tsp ground cinnamon
¼ tsp each ground allspice and
   ground nutmeg
4 pork loin chops, on the bone

For the rice:

1 tbsp vegetable oil
1 onion, peeled and finely chopped
1 celery stalk, trimmed and
   finely sliced
3 garlic cloves, peeled and crushed
2 bay leaves
225 g/8 oz long-grain white rice
475 ml/18 fl oz chicken or ham stock
sprigs of fresh flat-leaf parsley,
   to garnish

1   To make the jerk pork marinade, purée the onions, garlic, lime juice, molasses, soy sauce, ginger, chillies, cinnamon, allspice and nutmeg together in a food processor until smooth. Put the pork chops into a plastic or non-reactive dish and pour over the marinade, turning the chops to coat. Marinate in the refrigerator for at least 1 hour or overnight.

2   Drain the beans and place in a large saucepan with about 2 litres/3½ pints cold water. Bring to the boil and boil rapidly for 10 minutes. Reduce the heat, cover and simmer gently, for 1 hour until tender, adding more water, if necessary. When cooked, drain well and mash roughly.

3   Heat the oil for the rice in a saucepan with a tight-fitting lid and add the onion, celery and garlic. Cook gently for 5 minutes until softened. Add the bay leaves, rice and stock and stir. Bring to the boil, cover and cook very gently for 10 minutes. Add the beans and stir well again. Cook for a further 5 minutes, then remove from the heat.

4   Heat a griddle pan until almost smoking. Remove the pork chops from the marinade, scraping off any surplus and add to the hot pan. Cook for 5–8 minutes on each side, or until cooked. Garnish with the parsley and serve immediately with the rice.

Pork Chop Hotpot

INGREDIENTS

Serves 4

4 pork chops
flour for dusting
225 g/8 oz shallots, peeled
2 garlic cloves, peeled
50 g/2 oz sun-dried tomatoes
2 tbsp olive oil
400 g can plum tomatoes
150 ml/¼ pint red wine
150 ml/¼ pint chicken stock
3 tbsp tomato purée
2 tbsp freshly chopped oregano
salt and freshly ground black pepper
fresh oregano leaves, to garnish

To serve:

freshly cooked new potatoes
French beans

1 Preheat the oven to 190°C/375°F/Gas Mark 5, 10 minutes before cooking. Trim the pork chops, removing any excess fat, wipe with a clean, damp cloth, then dust with a little flour and reserve. Cut the shallots in half if large. Chop the garlic and slice the sun-dried tomatoes.

2 Heat the olive oil in a large casserole dish and cook the pork chops for about 5 minutes, turning occasionally during cooking, until browned all over. Using a slotted spoon, carefully lift out of the dish and reserve. Add the shallots and cook for 5 minutes, stirring occasionally.

3 Return the pork chops to the casserole dish and scatter with the garlic and sun-dried tomatoes, then pour over the can of tomatoes with their juice.

4 Blend the red wine, stock and tomato purée together and add the chopped oregano. Season to taste with salt and pepper, then pour over the pork chops and bring to a gentle boil. Cover with a close-fitting lid and cook in the preheated oven for 1 hour, or until the pork chops are tender. Adjust the seasoning to taste, then scatter with a few oregano leaves and serve immediately with freshly cooked potatoes and French beans.

TASTY TIP

Choose bone-in chops for this recipe. Remove any excess fat and rind before cooking.

Spiced Couscous & Vegetables

INGREDIENTS

Serves 4

1 tbsp olive oil
1 large shallot, peeled and
   finely chopped
1 garlic clove, peeled and
   finely chopped
1 small red pepper, deseeded and cut
   into strips
1 small yellow pepper, deseeded and
   cut into strips
1 small aubergine, diced
1 tsp each turmeric, ground cumin,
   ground cinnamon and paprika
2 tsp ground coriander
large pinch saffron strands
2 tomatoes, peeled, deseeded
   and diced
2 tbsp lemon juice
225 g/8 oz couscous
225 ml/8 fl oz vegetable stock
2 tbsp raisins
2 tbsp whole almonds
2 tbsp freshly chopped parsley
2 tbsp freshly chopped coriander
salt and freshly ground black pepper

1 Heat the oil in a large frying pan and add the shallot and garlic and cook for 2–3 minutes until softened. Add the peppers and aubergine and reduce the heat.

2 Cook for 8–10 minutes until the vegetables are tender, adding a little water if necessary.

3 Test a piece of aubergine to ensure it is cooked through. Add all the spices and cook for a further minute, stirring.

4 Increase the heat and add the tomatoes and lemon juice. Cook for 2–3 minutes until the tomatoes have started to break down. Remove from the heat and leave to cool slightly.

5 Meanwhile, put the couscous into a large bowl. Bring the stock to the boil in a saucepan, then pour over the couscous. Stir well and cover with a clean tea towel.

6 Leave to stand for 7–8 minutes until all the stock is absorbed and the couscous is tender.

7 Uncover the couscous and fluff with a fork. Stir in the vegetable and spice mixture along with the raisins, almonds, parsley and coriander. Season to taste with salt and pepper and serve.

Chinese Salad with Soy & Ginger Dressing

INGREDIENTS

Serves 4

1 head of Chinese cabbage
200 g can water chestnuts, drained
6 spring onions, trimmed
4 ripe but firm cherry tomatoes
125 g/4 oz mangetout
125 g/4 oz beansprouts
2 tbsp freshly chopped coriander

For the soy and ginger dressing:

2 tbsp sunflower oil
4 tbsp light soy sauce
2.5 cm/1 inch piece root ginger,
  peeled and finely grated
zest and juice of 1 lemon
salt and freshly ground black pepper
crusty white bread, to serve

1 Rinse and finely shred the Chinese cabbage and place in a serving dish.

2 Slice the water chestnuts into small slivers and cut the spring onions diagonally into 2.5 cm/1 inch lengths, then split lengthways into thin strips.

3 Cut the tomatoes in half and then slice each half into 3 wedges and reserve.

4 Simmer the mangetout in boiling water for 2 minutes until beginning to soften, drain and cut in half diagonally.

5 Arrange the water chestnuts, spring onions, mangetout, tomatoes and beansprouts on top of the shredded Chinese cabbage. Garnish with the freshly chopped coriander.

6 Make the dressing by whisking all the ingredients together in a small bowl until mixed thoroughly. Serve with the bread and the salad.

2

3

5

Stuffed Tomatoes with Grilled Polenta

INGREDIENTS

Serves 4

For the polenta:

300 ml/½ pint vegetable stock
salt and freshly ground black pepper
50 g/2 oz quick-cook polenta
15 g/½ oz butter

For the stuffed tomatoes:

4 large tomatoes
1 tbsp olive oil
1 garlic clove, peeled and crushed
1 bunch spring onions, trimmed and
    finely chopped
2 tbsp freshly chopped parsley
2 tbsp freshly chopped basil
2 slices Parma ham, cut into
    thin slivers
50 g/2 oz fresh white breadcrumbs
snipped chives, to garnish

1 Preheat the grill just before cooking. To make the polenta, pour the stock into a saucepan. Add a pinch of salt and bring to the boil. Pour in the polenta in a fine stream, stirring all the time. Simmer for about 15 minutes, or until very thick. Stir in the butter and add a little pepper. Turn the polenta out onto a chopping board and spread to a thickness of just over 1 cm/½ inch. Cool, cover with clingfilm and chill in the refrigerator for 30 minutes.

2 To make the stuffed tomatoes, cut the tomatoes in half then scoop out the seeds and press through a fine sieve to extract the juices. Season the insides of the tomatoes with salt and pepper and reserve.

3 Heat the olive oil in a saucepan and gently fry the garlic and spring onions for 3 minutes. Add the tomatoes' juices, bubble for 3–4 minutes, until most of the liquid has evaporated. Stir in the herbs, Parma ham and a little black pepper with half the breadcrumbs. Spoon into the hollowed out tomatoes and reserve.

4 Cut the polenta into 5 cm/2 inch squares, then cut each in half diagonally to make triangles. Put the triangles onto a piece of tinfoil on the grill rack and grill for 4–5 minutes on each side, until golden. Cover and keep warm.

5 Grill the tomatoes under a medium-hot grill for about 4 minutes – any exposed Parma ham will become crisp. Sprinkle with the remaining breadcrumbs and grill for 1–2 minutes, or until the breadcrumbs are golden brown. Garnish with snipped chives and serve immediately with the grilled polenta.

Three Tomato Pizza

INGREDIENTS

Serves 2–4

1 quantity pizza dough
3 plum tomatoes
8 cherry tomatoes
6 sun-dried tomatoes
pinch of sea salt
1 tbsp freshly chopped basil
2 tbsp extra-virgin olive oil
125 g/4 oz buffalo mozzarella
  cheese, sliced
freshly ground black pepper
fresh basil leaves, to garnish

FOOD FACT

Buffalo mozzarella is considered the king of mozzarellas. It uses buffalo milk, which results in the cheese tasting extremely mild and creamy. A good mozzarella should come in liquid to keep it moist and should tear easily into chunks.

1 Preheat the oven to 220°C/425°F/Gas Mark 7. Place a baking sheet into the oven to heat up.

2 Divide the prepared pizza dough into 4 equal pieces.

3 Roll out one-quarter of the pizza dough onto a lightly floured board to form a 20.5 cm/8 inch round.

4 Lightly cover the 3 remaining pieces of dough with clingfilm.

5 Roll out the other 3 pieces into rounds, one at a time. While rolling out any piece of dough, keep the others covered with the clingfilm.

6 Slice the plum tomatoes, halve the cherry tomatoes and chop the sun-dried tomatoes into small pieces.

7 Place a few pieces of each type of tomato onto each pizza base then season to taste with the sea salt.

8 Sprinkle with the chopped basil and drizzle with the olive oil. Place a few slices of mozzarella on each pizza and season with black pepper.

9 Transfer the pizza onto the heated baking sheet and cook for 15–20 minutes, or until the cheese is golden brown and bubbling. Garnish with the basil leaves and serve immediately.

3

7

8

Index